CONTENTS

What Is the Power and Why Do I Need It? 5

Lord, Help Me Know You Better 15

Lord, Help Me Get Free of Past Mistakes 27

Lord, Help Me Forgive Others 37

Lord, Help Me Do What's Right 47

Lord, Help Me Stand Strong Against Bad
    Influences 57

Lord, Help Me Take Control of My Mind 69

Lord, Help Me Understand Your Word 79

Lord, Help Me Be Free from Peer Pressure 89

Lord, Help Me Have Good Relationships 101

Lord, Help Me Praise You at All Times 109

11 Lord, Help Me Find Your Purpose for My Life 117

12 Lord, Help Me Make Wise Choices 127

13 Lord, Help Me Get Rid of Negative Emotions 135

14 Lord, Help Me Resist Temptation 147

15 Lord, Help Me Be Strong When Bad Things
Happen 155

16 Lord, Help Me Be Safe 163

17 Lord, Help Me Speak Words That Bring Life 171

18 Lord, Help Me Have Faith for the Impossible 181

19 Lord, Help Me Know Your Will for My Life 189

20 Lord, Help Me Move Into the Future You Have
for Me 197

THE POWER OFA Praying® Teen

STORMIE OMARTIAN

HARVEST HOUSE PUBLISHERS
EUGENE, OREGON

Unless otherwise indicated, all Scripture quotations are taken from the New King James Version. Copyright © 1982 by Thomas Nelson, Inc. Used by permission. All rights reserved.

Verses marked NIV are taken from the HOLY BIBLE, NEW INTERNATIONAL VERSION®. NIV®. Copyright © 1973, 1978, 1984 by the International Bible Society. Used by permission of Zondervan. All rights reserved.

Verses marked ASV are taken from the American Standard Version of the Bible.

Cover by Koechel Peterson & Associates, Inc., Minneapolis, Minnesota

THE POWER OF A PRAYING is a registered trademark of The Hawkins Children's LLC. Harvest House Publishers, Inc., is the exclusive licensee of the federally registered trademark THE POWER OF A PRAYING.

THE POWER OF A PRAYING® TEEN
Copyright © 2005 by Stormie Omartian
Published by Harvest House Publishers
Eugene, Oregon 97402
www.harvesthousepublishers.com

Library of Congress Cataloging-in-Publication Data

Omartian, Stormie.
  The power of a praying teen / Stormie Omartian.
    p. cm.
  ISBN 978-0-7369-0190-1 (pbk.)
  ISBN 978-0-7369-3323-0 (eBook)
  1. Christian teenagers—Religious life. 2. Prayer—Christianity. I. Title.
  BV4531.3.O43 2005
  248.8'3—dc22   2005009384

All rights reserved. No part of this publication may be reproduced, stored in a retrieval system, or transmitted in any form or by any means—electronic, mechanical, digital, photocopy, recording, or any other—except for brief quotations in printed reviews, without the prior permission of the publisher.

Printed in the United States of America

15 16 17 18 19 / BP-MS / 25 24 23

WHAT IS THE POWER and Why Do I Need It?

IF YOU ARE A TEENAGER, THEN YOU'RE IN a unique position to be able to affect your world in a powerful way. That's because you are part of a world that is intense, in-your-face, and in some ways very small. It's small because people who are *not* teenagers don't get to be part of it in the way that *you* do. You are able to see up close all the things that are good and bad in your world—the things you wish would never end and the things you know that need to be changed.

You, your life, and your world can be affected far more than you ever dreamed possible by simply praying about them every day.

Who, Me? I Don't Have Time to Pray

As a teenager, you have a busy life. There has never been more pressure to learn, improve, and succeed. And there have never been more opportunities to do it. You may feel you don't have *time* to pray. If so, you're not alone. Many people feel that way. Life is filled with countless things that are designed to keep us too busy to pray. But when we don't spend time with God every day in prayer, we miss hearing His voice speaking to our heart and leading us in important ways. It can cause us to miss out on many of the good things He has for our life.

The Main Things I Pray About Are:

- Good health for me and my family
- That I will be a success in life
- That I will be free of temptation
- That there will be peace in the world
- That God will save my generation (Ages 16-19)

I have found a way for you to pray about every aspect of your life that will keep you focused on who God is and who He made you to be. And this is very important, because when a person does not know who God really is, and who He made them to be, they can end up making bad decisions and never experiencing all God has for them.

This way of praying will take the problems off of your own shoulders and put the burden of them on God. He not only wants to carry them for you, He also wants to lift you *above* difficult situations so you can see things from *His* perspective. When you can do that, you will be able to tell what is true and what is a lie. Far too often we believe things that are not true about ourselves and our situations, and this can limit or even paralyze us to the point where we can't move forward like we should. Seeing the truth as God reveals it sets us free.

Most of all, this kind of praying will help you get really close to God. And that's where you want to be. When you are close to God, you can share the deepest feelings and desires of your heart. And your heart can hear Him guiding you on the path He has for you, revealing to you the wonderful plans He has for your future.

God Has a Purpose for Your Life

The most important thing you ever need to understand is that God *created* you, He *loves* you, He is *committed* to you, and He has a *great purpose* for your life. But you have to not only *believe* this in your head, you have to *know* it in your heart. And it is only through a close relationship with God that you can truly know all this.

The way to *begin* a close relationship with God is to receive His Son, Jesus. Simply ask Jesus to come into your life. Then get ahold of a Bible and start reading it. (Check out different translations for one that is perfect for you.) Be sure you're hanging out with people who know the Lord. How can you become all God created you to be if you are constantly thrust into a world that wants you to be molded into *its* image? The people who have the greatest influence in your life should be those who know God. Look for them at school. But especially look for them in a good church, because there they can give you the solid support you need to grow in your relationship with the Lord.

Having a close relationship with God doesn't mean that you will never have problems, but it does mean that when you do, He will be there to help you. He will calm the storms in your life when things get rough. He will take the tough challenges you face and either transform them, enable you to rise above them, or help you walk through them successfully.

But all these things don't just happen. Not without prayer.

When you walk close to God by reading His Word and spending time with Him every day in prayer, you will find out who you really are and who you were created to be. You will understand God's purpose for your life.

What Is Prayer and Why Does It Work?

Prayer is simply communicating with God. It's talking to Him and sharing whatever is on your heart. It's telling Him how you feel about your *life* and how you feel about *Him*. It's sharing with God all the things you see that are wrong and how you would like them to be changed. And it's letting Him speak to *your* heart about how He feels about *you* and what His plans and purposes are for *your* life.

When you pray often, you are focused on who God is and who you are in relation to Him. When you talk to God, He begins to show you more and more who He made you to be and what He wants you to do. And that is one of the most important things you will need to know in your life.

Enough About You, Let's Talk About Me

This book will help you learn how to pray for yourself and your life, and for other people and situations as well. It's the book I wish I'd had when I was a teenager. If I would have known all these things, I wouldn't have gotten into so much trouble and wasted so many years of my life searching for things I couldn't have. I wouldn't have spent time striving to be something I wasn't created to be. I wouldn't have suffered the discouragement, depression, frustration, anxiety, and hopelessness that I did. I would have been spared a lot of misery and pain.

When I was a teenager, my family and I lived in a part of town that wasn't as nice as where all the other kids lived. It wasn't nice at all. The other kids lived in houses that were large, new, and well kept. Mine was small, old, and run-down. They came from wealthy families. Mine was poor. They wore better clothes, drove nicer cars, and went places on vacation. What few clothes I had to wear

My Prayer to God
Lord, help me go through this wonderful life You have given me. Give me everything I need and help me spiritually, emotionally, and physically.
(Age 13)

were worn out, our car was so old and beat up it barely ran, and we never went anywhere. They ate well, stayed healthier, and lived better. I often went to bed hungry, was sick most of the time, and stayed miserable. They looked forward to life; I dreaded every day and wanted to die more often than I wanted to live.

If I had known the Lord back then, I would have been able to come to Him about all the needs in my life. I would have felt His presence and His power helping me through each day and taking away my hurt and loneliness. I would have stopped being embarrassed about who I was and been grateful for who God was making me to be. I would have learned to live God's way and stayed out of trouble. I would have recognized my gifts and talents sooner and developed them, instead of beating myself up for not being who I thought I should be. I would have understood God's will for my life and not gotten off the path and wasted so many years trying to figure life out and find my way.

I'll tell you more about my story throughout this book, and I hope you will learn enough from it to avoid the mistakes and the misery I had to endure.

Why Is It So Hard to Pray Sometimes?

Do you ever feel like it's hard to pray? If so, you're not alone. I have felt that way too. In fact, everyone feels that way at one time or another, no matter how old they are or how long they have known the Lord.

There are many different reasons why we find praying difficult. One reason is that we are not sure we're saying the right things. We think we have to sound like a preacher or that we have to use just the right words. We're afraid that we might not say things right enough or good enough. Or we are not praying long enough or hard enough.

Sometimes we think that God isn't really hearing our prayers at all. Or perhaps our prayers are not important to Him. Or He is too busy to listen. Or we believe that the issues we want to pray about are so big and we are so small, how can our prayers possibly make any difference? We feel powerless to pray in a way that can bring about any kind of change. We don't understand how powerful our prayers are and what can be accomplished when we pray.

Do you find it easier to pray for other people than it is to pray for yourself? I know I have felt that way. I could pray for my friends, family, and people I had never even met who I heard about in the news far easier than I could pray for my own needs. Why is that?

For one thing, the needs of other people were easy for me to figure out. Mine were often complicated and not easy to talk about. Often I just didn't have a clue as to how to pray about a particular situation. Or the circumstances were so overwhelming that my prayers were nothing more than a basic cry for help. Sometimes I just thought I could not pray a prayer that God would want to listen to. I have since found out that none of that is true.

The truth is that God is not looking for someone to pray who is perfect and who says the perfect "Christianese" words in the perfect way. He is looking for someone who has a heart of love for *Him*. He doesn't measure your prayers by how long you pray. He measures them by how important they are to you. He knows what is going on in your heart, and He cares about the things *you* care about. That's because He cares about *you*. What is important to *you* is important to *Him*. That's why He wants you to come to Him with the things that are important to you.

You may be thinking, *If God knows what is in my heart and He cares about me, then why do I need to pray? Why doesn't He just give me what I need without my having to ask Him?*

The answer is because He wants you to *come* to Him, to be *close* to Him, to *talk* to Him, and to *depend* on Him. He wants to talk to you about the things that are important to *Him* so that they can become important to *you*. He wants to take you to places you can't get to without Him. He wants to do great things through you, but you have to walk close to Him in order for that to happen. When you understand all of this, it makes praying a lot easier.

What Can I Do When I Feel Powerless?

Have you ever felt that your life is out of control and you are powerless to do anything about it? Do you sometimes feel so pressured by outside circumstances or internal emotions that you think you're going to explode? Have you ever felt as if your life is stuck in one place and you are going nowhere? Or worse yet, you are going backward? Do you ever experience feelings of emptiness or frustration? Have you wondered if you can actually move into the destiny God has for you? Most people feel those things, especially people your age. But the good news is that God has a way for you to pray that will empower you to rise above all those feelings.

> **I Prayed and God Answered**
> I asked God to help me in my relationship with Him. I didn't pray a lot and now I pray daily. I sometimes forget to read my Bible, but I've improved.
> (Age 14)

Have you ever wanted to do something great—something that would make a difference in this world—but you didn't know what to do or how to do it? If you have, take comfort in knowing that this is the way God wants you to feel. He, too, wants you to do something great that will make a difference in this world, but He wants you to seek Him for the ability and the power to do it. Too often we try to do things on our own and become discouraged when they don't happen the way we hoped they would.

What we need is a power far greater than ourselves. But there is only one power in the world great enough to help us rise above ourselves and our limitations and our circumstances, and that is the power of God.

How Do I Move in the Power of God?

The greatest thing that happens when we invite Jesus into our lives is that God's Holy Spirit comes to live inside of us. Because we have His Holy Spirit in us, we will never be alone and we will always have access to everything we need. That means every time we pray to God in Jesus' name, His power is released to work in whatever situation we are praying about. When we deny the Holy Spirit's power, we become like those people the Bible talks about who live "having a form of godliness but denying its power" (2 Timothy 3:5).

Without God's power, we can't rise above our limitations. We can't stand strong in the face of all we come up against every day.

God wants us to understand "what is the exceeding greatness of His power toward us who believe" (Ephesians 1:19). He wants us to see that "we have received, not the spirit of the world, but the Spirit who is from God, that we might know the things that have been freely given to us by God" (1 Corinthians 2:12). That means that because we have the Spirit of God living in us, we will be able to experience all the things God has for us. Isn't that good news?

I can't make you understand the power of God or the way the Holy Spirit wants to work in you. That is beyond my capabilities and authority in your life. But you don't need me to convince you because the Holy Spirit will do that Himself. Jesus said, "The Helper, the Holy Spirit, whom the Father will send in My name, He will teach you all things" (John 14:26). The Holy Spirit will show you.

Once you have made Jesus the Lord of your life, you will come to know Him as the one "who is able to do exceedingly abundantly above all that we ask or think, according to the power that works in us" (Ephesians 3:20). This means that because of God's Holy Spirit in you—His power in you—He can do more in your life than you can ever think to ask for. He can do more than you can even imagine. How great is that?

The Way It Works

This book will help you pray about the different issues of your life. Just take it a chapter at a time. At the end of each chapter is a section called "Prayer Power," which is a prayer you can pray to get you started. As you're praying, other things will come to your mind to include.

After that is a section called "Word Power." These are important promises from God's Word that relate to that particular subject. As you read each one, think about what that particular promise means specifically for you and your life. The last section of each chapter is called "Giving It Some Further Thought." These are questions for you to answer and thoughts for you to complete that will help you learn to pray about those things.

> **I Pray for Others When:**
> - I am worried about them
> - They help me
> - I think about them
> - They are sad
> - I get the chance
>
> (Ages 13-15)

Throughout all the chapters are little boxes containing the thoughts, prayers, and opinions of teenagers. I decided to keep all of these anonymous because many of them are very personal and I wanted to protect the privacy of everyone who took the survey. It is equally divided between male and female contributors. The teens themselves did not *take* the survey anonymously, however. I saw and spoke with them personally, and they were very willing and open in their response because they believed their honesty could help other teens who are going through the same things they are experiencing.

Time to Move On

When you walk with the Lord, you are never standing still. You are either going forward or you're sliding back. You are either becoming more like Christ every day or you're becoming less like Him. That is the reason I wrote this book. I want you to keep moving forward by spending time with the Lord every day. I want you to learn to love God and live His way so you can receive all He has for you. When you live according to God's Word and by the power of His Holy Spirit, then you can trust that the Lord is working His perfect will in your life and you are becoming all He made you to be.

Prayer Power

Lord, You have said in Your Word that Your Holy Spirit helps us to pray (Romans 8:26). I invite You, Holy Spirit, to teach me how to pray. Show me the things I need to know. Give me the faith I need to believe that You will always hear me and You will answer in Your way and in Your time. Thank You, Lord, that You sent Your Holy Spirit so I could live in power and be used powerfully by You (1 Corinthians 1:18). Help me do that. I need Your power to enable me to live the way You want me to so that I can become all You created me to be. In Jesus' name I pray.

chapter 1

LORD, HELP ME, Know You Better

Before I came to know the Lord, I was involved in all kinds of occult practices and Eastern and New Age religions. In each one of these I was trying to find God and discover some purpose for why I was alive. I became desperate to find a way out of the emotional pain, fear, anxiety, and depression I had experienced nearly every day since I was a child. I thought that there must be a God, and if I could just be good enough to get close to Him, maybe He would give meaning to my life and then I could feel better about myself.

Of course that didn't happen because the gods I chased after were distant and cold. And this depressed me even more because I was raised by a mother who was distant and cold. She was also physically violent, verbally abusive, frightening, and cruel. She locked me in a closet for long periods of time, and that made me

The Hardest Thing About Prayer Is:
- Admitting my sins
- Praying from my heart
- Keeping my eyes closed
- Not being selfish
- Nothing. It's easy!

(Ages 13-15)

very afraid and sad. I realized later that she was seriously mentally ill, and because she never received any medical help, she only grew worse and worse as time went on.

I eventually forgave my mother for all the things I suffered because of her, but I still had extremely bad memories of my childhood. I had always hidden that part of my life from other people, but especially when I was a teenager. Being different was not a good thing at that age, and it certainly wasn't good to be different in a *negative* way like that. The pain I felt as a teenager became like an avalanche that crashed in on me until it seemed as though I were suffocating under the weight of it. The hopelessness, depression, and despair I felt became so unbearable that I had constant thoughts of suicide.

Once I was in my twenties and out on my own, I tried everything I could think of to get out of my misery, but nothing worked. I took drugs to the point that I nearly killed myself a couple of times from an overdose. I drank alcohol to try to numb the pain, but it only made me feel sick and confused. Finally, at the lowest point in my life, I was 28 years old and had done everything I knew to find a way out of the pain I constantly felt. I wanted to die and was planning a way to kill myself.

It was at that very time that my friend Terry saw I wasn't doing very well, so she asked me to go with her to meet her pastor. She was a Christian and I wasn't; I hesitated. I was afraid I would have to tell them both about my mother or my problems, or reveal the terrible things I had done. I didn't want anyone to know. But I was also desperate to find a reason to live, and so I went.

Terry's pastor, Pastor Jack, met us at a popular restaurant in town. We ate and sat there for two hours while he told me about

Jesus. When Pastor Jack talked about Him, He didn't seem like the cold, judgmental gods I had been reading about in my books on the occult and Eastern religions. Pastor Jack told me that if I received Jesus as my Savior, I could begin a close walk with God that would change my life forever. He would help me find peace and restoration. He would show me His purpose for my life, and it would be better than anything I had ever imagined.

Pastor Jack gave me three books to read. One was about the reality of evil. My occult practices had taught me that there was no evil. The second book was on the power of the Holy Spirit. I had never known about that kind of power, and I was fascinated that I could have access to it when I received Jesus. The third book was the Gospel of John in a small book form. It told about the life of Jesus and who He was and what He taught. Pastor Jack asked me to come to his office with Terry after I had read the books, and then I could let him know what I thought of them.

I went home, put my suicide plans on hold, and read all three books in just a few days. When I went back with Terry the following week, I told Pastor Jack that I believed what I had read was the truth. He asked me if I was ready to receive Jesus as my Savior, and I told him yes.

I Pray for Others When:

- They ask me to
- God tells me to
- They need help
- They are sick
- They are traveling
(Ages 13-15)

After I gave my life to the Lord, I could sense His Spirit working in me. I felt hope for the first time in my life, and I could see that I had a future. I didn't know exactly what it was, but I knew I had one. And that was a lot more than I could ever see before.

I could also see that there was a common thread in all those other occult practices and Eastern religions I had dabbled in previously. The similarity was that the gods of each of those religions had no power to save or transform a person and their life. But the

God of the Bible did. He is the one, true, living God, and when we receive His Son, Jesus, as our Savior, the Holy Spirit of God comes to dwell in us (John 14:16-17). It is by the power of His Spirit that He transforms us from the inside out and miraculously changes us and our circumstances and our lives.

I also learned that the God of the Bible can be known and that He *wants* to be close to us. That's why He is called Immanuel, which means "God *with* us." He comes close to *us* when we draw close to *Him* (James 4:8).

Everything You Need

I wish I could sit down and talk with you in person about your life. If I could, I would tell you that if you have received Jesus, the answer to everything you will ever need for your life is within you. That's because the Holy Spirit of God is in you. He promises to lead you in your life and teach you things you need to know. But you have to give your life to Him and be patient to let Him work in you in His way and in His timing.

To be *transformed* means to be changed permanently. It doesn't mean a *temporary* fix or a *little bit* changed. This is not about trying to be good enough in order to get God to love you. God already loves you. He loved you first. He is just waiting for you to love Him. This is about coming to know Jesus, who is perfect, and letting His perfect love change you and help you do the right things. This is about a close walk with God and the great things that will happen in you because of it.

What Everyone Wants

Everyone wants to be loved, but no one will ever be able to love us as much as God can. Only God can meet your needs all the time—and then only when you have a *close* relationship with Him. No person can ever touch you as deeply as God can. No one can ever know you as well. Whenever you feel an emptiness inside of you that you want those closest to you to fill and they just aren't doing that, remember that this emptiness is put there by God. He wants you to come close to Him so *He* can fill it.

God wants you to want Him. And when you realize that it is really *Him* that you want, it frees you to identify the longings, loneliness, or emptiness inside of you as a sign that you need to draw near to God and ask Him to fill you with more of Himself. But this deep relationship with God that we all want, whether we know it's what we want at the time or not, doesn't just happen. It has to be sought after. We have to *pray* for a deeper relationship with God. We have to pray that our walk with God is not shallow.

Five Ways to Tell if Your Walk with God Is Shallow

1. *If you love the Lord only for what He can do for you,* then your walk with Him is shallow. If you love Him enough to ask what *you* can do for *Him,* then your relationship is *growing deeper.*

2. *If you only pray to God when things are tough or you need something,* then your walk with Him is shallow. If you pray to Him often just because you love to be close to Him, then your relationship with God is *growing deeper.*

3. *If you get mad at God or disappointed in Him when He doesn't do what you want,* then your walk with Him is shallow. If you can praise God and pray to Him no matter what is going on in your life, then your relationship with Him is *growing deeper.*

4. *If you praise God only because of what He does for you,* then your walk with Him is shallow. If you also praise Him because of who He is, then your relationship with Him is *growing deeper.*

5. *If you feel you have to beg God or twist His arm to get Him to answer your prayers,* then your walk with Him is shallow. If

you believe that God *wants* to answer your prayers according to His will, then your relationship with Him is *growing deeper*.

Spending Time Alone with God

We can never draw close to God and get to know Him well if we don't spend time alone with Him. It's in those private times with God that we are refreshed and strengthened. That's when we can better see our lives from His perspective and discover what is really important. That's where we understand who God really is and all that He has for us.

Jesus Himself spent time alone with God. If anyone could get away with not doing it, surely it would have been Jesus. How much more important must it be for us?

I Think of God As:
- Someone who listens to me
- Someone who loves me
- Someone I can talk to
- Someone who is always good
- Someone who leads me
  (Ages 13-15)

I know that finding time alone to pray to God can be difficult. But if you will make it a priority, you'll see answers to your prayers like never before. Remember, if you haven't been praying much, you can't expect things to change overnight. When someone tries to get an enormous ocean liner turned around and headed in a different direction, it doesn't happen the moment they begin steering. In fact, they may hardly see any change at all at first. It's the same way with prayer. Prayer can turn your life around, but it doesn't always happen the moment you say your first words. If you haven't been praying very much, or not at all, you can't expect things to change immediately. It may take a time of continued prayer before you actually see the scenery of your life begin to change. This is normal, so don't give up. You will soon be heading full speed in a new direction.

Far too often people give up just before they see the answers to their prayers. Just remember that this is not a short trip around the harbor. It's a lifelong voyage to meet your destiny. Giving up is not an option.

Naming Names

Do you ever have trouble remembering names? I know I do. Especially when I meet a lot of people at one time. It's easier to remember faces than it is to remember names. With God it's a different situation. He has only one face, but many, many names. The reason for that is there's so much to know about God that we need all those names to help us remember. In other words, if we don't know all of His names, we may not fully understand all the aspects of who He is.

God is referred to by many different names in the Bible, but sometimes we have trouble just remembering a few of the basic ones. We may forget one just when we most need to remember it. For example, we may think of God as

> **I Prayed and God Answered**
> I prayed when I got sick and God healed me.
> (Age 13)

our Provider, but forget that He is also our Protector. Or we may remember Him as our heavenly Father, but forget that He is also our Friend. We may think of God as our Savior, but forget that He is also our Deliverer.

Each of God's names in the Bible represents a way He wants us to trust Him:

Do you trust Him to be your Strength (Psalm 18:1)?

Is He your Peace (Ephesians 2:14)?

Is He the Lifter of Your Head when you are down (Psalm 3:3)?

Is He your Wisdom (1 Corinthians 1:24)?

Is He your Counselor (Psalm 16:7)?

There is great power in each one of God's names. And when you speak them with faith and understanding, you come to know God better. The better you know Him, the more fantastic your life will be.

For example, God's name is always a safe place to run to anytime you need help. "The name of the LORD is a strong tower; the righteous run to it and are safe" (Proverbs 18:10).

If you are sick, run to your Healer.

If you are in need of something, run to your Provider.

If you are afraid, run to your Hiding Place.

By speaking one of His names, you invite Him to be that to you. Often there is so much we don't have in our lives simply because we don't see God as the answer to that need.

My Prayer to God
Lord, help me to remember to turn to you first when I am down.
(Age 15)

In the following list of God's names, I have included only 20. But there are hundreds more in His Word—the Bible. As you go through each of these names, thank God for being that to you. When you do, you will be amazed at how your faith will grow and how much closer to God you will feel. Knowing how much He has done for you will help you love Him more.

Twenty Names of God to Remember

1. God is my Healer (Psalm 103:3).
2. God is my Redeemer (Isaiah 59:20).
3. God is my Deliverer (Psalm 70:5).
4. God is my Strength (Psalm 43:2).
5. God is my Shelter (Joel 3:16).
6. God is my Friend (John 15:15).
7. God is my Restorer (Psalm 23:3).
8. God is my Father (Isaiah 9:6).
9. God is my Love (1 John 4:16).
10. God is my Hiding Place (Psalm 32:7).

11. God is my Resting Place (Jeremiah 50:6).
12. God is my Truth (John 16:13).
13. God is my Eternal Life (1 John 5:20).
14. God is my Lord Who Provides (Genesis 22:14).
15. God is my Lord of Peace (2 Thessalonians 3:16).
16. God is my Shield (Psalm 144:2).
17. God is my Helper (Hebrews 13:6).
18. God is my Counselor (Isaiah 9:6).
19. God is my Hope (Psalm 71:5).
20. God is my Comfort (Romans 15:5).

Read this list of names often, and every time you do, choose one name that you especially need God to be that day and then thank Him for being that to you. And whenever you are reading your Bible and you come across a name for God, underline it or jot it in the margin or add it to the list here. It will remind you of another aspect of who God is to you.

Prayer Power

Lord, I want to have a closer walk with You. I draw close to You right now and thank You that as I do, You are drawing closer to me just as You promised in Your Word (James 4:8). I want a deeper relationship with You. I want to know You in all the ways You can be known. I am open to everything You want to do in me and in my life. I don't want to limit You by neglecting to acknowledge You in every way possible. Teach me what I need to learn in order to know You better. I don't want to be a person who is "always learning and never able to come to the knowledge of the truth" (2 Timothy 3:7). I want to know the truth about who You are. Today I especially need to know You as my (say a name of the Lord that you most need Him to be to you today). Help me to trust that You will always be that to me. Help me to know You in that way more and more each day. In Jesus' name I pray.

WORD POWER

Draw near to God and He will draw near to you.

JAMES 4:8

Until now you have asked nothing in My name. Ask, and you will receive, that your joy may be full.

JOHN 16:24

It is your Father's good pleasure to give you the kingdom.

LUKE 12:32

1

The names of God that mean the most to me are:

2

The names of God that represent the ways in which I want to know God better are:

3

Write out a prayer telling God how you feel about Him and why you want to know Him better.

chapter 2

LORD, HELP ME

Get Free of Past Mistakes

BEFORE WE GO ANY FURTHER, let's get something straight: Everybody makes mistakes. Nobody is perfect. We are all capable of doing something wrong.

There! It's out in the open.

I said this because I don't want you to look at other people and think they have it all together and you don't. When you do that, you are putting impossibly high expectations on yourself.

This book is not about trying to live up to a certain standard. It's about letting *God* become your standard. It's not about trying to be perfect. It's surrendering your life to God and letting *Him* perfect you. It's not about finding ways to avoid God's judgment and then feeling like a failure if you don't do everything exactly right. It's about finding out how to experience God's love and grace. It's not about trying to be somebody you are not. It's about becoming who you really are. But in order to see these things happen, you have to be completely honest with yourself and with God about who you are at the moment.

The Hardest Thing About Prayer Is:

- When I don't see an immediate answer
- When I don't know what to pray about
- When I've done something wrong
- When something tragic happens
- When God shows me something about my life

(Ages 16-19)

As a teenager, you know that your life is just beginning. And you want to live a successful life. You want to know how life works best so you can live that way and have the best possible life. But since everybody makes mistakes, this means that you probably have already made mistakes and will make them again in the future.

Often when we do things wrong, we know that's what we're doing. We know if we've lied or disobeyed a law. But sometimes we make mistakes without knowing it. We didn't realize that what we were doing was wrong in God's eyes because we didn't know enough about God's ways. (More about that in chapter 4.) Whether or not we know what we're doing is wrong, it is still sin. Sin is an old archery term that means missing the mark. If we don't get things right on target in our lives, we miss the mark God has for us. And then we don't get to experience all the good things He has planned for our future.

Sin destroys us. We may think we can get away with not living God's way, but sin will always bring destruction into our lives. The good news is that God loves us so much that He has given us a way out of the destruction that comes because of our sins. It's called confession.

Confession is something you can do anytime you come to God. It's telling God what you have done and saying you're sorry. You're not telling Him something He doesn't know. He already knows! He wants to know that *you* know. And that you have a heart to change.

Having a change of heart is called repentance. In order to do those two things—confess and repent—you have to look at your life closely. You have to be brave enough to say, "Lord, show me what is in my heart and mind and life that shouldn't be there. Show me where I am missing the mark. Help me to see the truth about myself. Help me change."

It takes courage to pray a prayer like that. Sometimes we're afraid to let God expose our heart because of what He might reveal inside of it. But we can *ask* Him for the *courage* to do it. In order to receive all that God has for you, you have to be willing to clear the slate with Him. You have to invite Him to expose any sin in your life and let Him create a clean heart in you.

God doesn't want you walking around feeling guilty. He wants you to get sin out in the open before Him so you can be free of it. Carrying around the guilt of past mistakes will limit what God wants to do in your life. And it will make you feel bad about yourself. Guilt is not attractive. And it doesn't feel good. Don't let it be part of your life. It's not worth it. If you want to get free of the guilt of all past mistakes, then be willing to do these two things:

I Prayed and God Answered

I was dating a guy behind my parents' backs. I asked God to help me make the right choices. The guy came up to me and said it was over. I wasn't hurt or anything.

I just knew God did that. And now I have given up dating.
(Age 13)

1. *Confess* to God any sins of thought or action that you know you have done or that He shows you when you ask Him.
2. *Repent* of the things you have just confessed.

True Confession

Don't think just because you're not a serial killer or have never robbed a bank that you don't have any sin to confess. Don't think because you have walked with the Lord for a number of years and go to church every Sunday that you have nothing for which you need to repent. Sin doesn't have to be glaring and obvious in order for it to be sin.

For example, have you ever doubted that God can do what He promises in His Word? Doubt is a sin.

Have you ever said anything to someone about another person that isn't exactly flattering? Gossip is a sin.

> **My Prayer to God**
> Lord, I don't know how to pray very well, but I need strength to resist temptation.
> (Age 18)

Have you ever avoided someone because you thought they might ask something of you that you didn't want to give? Selfishness is a sin.

You can try hard, but you can't avoid sin all the time. That's why confession is crucial. When we don't confess our sins, faults, or errors, they separate us from God. And we don't get our prayers answered. The Bible says, "Your iniquities have separated you from your God; and your sins have hidden His face from you, so that He will not hear" (Isaiah 59:2).

That's a frightening thought. Imagine God putting His fingers in His ears and saying, "La la la la la la" over and over really loud when you pray.

When we don't confess our sins, we end up trying to hide ourselves from God, just like Adam and Eve did in the Garden of Eden. We feel like we can't face Him. But the problem with attempting to hide from God is that it's impossible. The Bible says that God knows everything we do. Even the things we said and thought in secret. "There is nothing covered that will not be revealed, nor hidden that will not be known. Therefore whatever you have spoken in the dark will be heard in the light, and what you have spoken in the ear in inner rooms will be proclaimed on the housetops" (Luke 12:2-3).

The Bible also says, "There is no creature hidden from His sight, but all things are naked and open to the eyes of Him to whom we must give account" (Hebrews 4:13). That's scary too.

If each of us will have to give an account of our actions and thoughts, the quicker we get it straight with God, the better. In fact, the sooner we deal with the sins we can see, the sooner God can reveal to us the ones we can't. And only God knows how much of that is residing in each of us.

There is always a consequence for sin. King David described it best when he wrote of his own unconfessed sin: "There is no soundness in my flesh because of Your anger, nor any health in my bones because of my sin. For my iniquities have gone over my head; like a heavy burden they are too heavy for me" (Psalm 38:3-4).

> **I Believe in Prayer Because:**
> - I have had my prayers answered before
> - I have seen it change a situation
> - I have experienced miracles
> - It has helped me through the hardest times
> - It makes the impossible seem possible
>
> (Ages 16-19)

Have you ever felt that way about something you have done? I know I have. It felt as though there was a heaviness in my heart and on my head that took away all my energy and life. Sin definitely doesn't make me feel good about myself.

I remember having resentment toward a person once because of words he had said that hurt me deeply. As long as I held on to the hurt and resentment, I felt physically ill. I didn't want to confess these feelings because I thought they were justified and *he* was the one who was wrong. But I finally realized that all sin is sin, so I confessed my resentment to God. The moment I did that, the feeling of sickness left my body.

I Think of God As:

- An Almighty Ruler who is in control of all situations
- A Judge who decides if I'm worthy to have my prayer answered
- A Listener who I can talk to and confide in
- The only One who really knows me
- A Father who loves unconditionally

(Ages 16-19)

Nothing is heavier than sin. We don't realize how heavy it is until the day we feel its weight crushing our souls. We don't see how destructive it is until we smash into the wall that has gone up between us and God because of it. That's why it's best to confess every sin as soon as we are aware of it so we can get our hearts clean immediately.

Confessing is more than just apologizing. Anyone can do that. We all know people who are good apologizers. The reason they are so good at it is because they get so much practice. They say "I'm sorry" over and over again, but they never change their ways. And their confessions don't mean anything. True confession means admitting to God in full detail what you have done and then fully repenting of it.

What Does It Mean to Repent?

It's one thing to recognize when you have done something wrong; it's another to be so saddened by what you've done that you are determined to never do it again. That's repentance.

Confession means we recognize we have done wrong and admit our sin. Repentance means we are sorry about our sin to the point of grief, and we have turned and walked away from it.

Repenting of something doesn't necessarily mean we will never do that thing again. It means we don't *intend* to ever do it again. So if you find that you have to confess the same sin again after you have only recently confessed and repented of it, then do it. Don't let the enemy saddle you with guilt and ride on your back, telling you how you have failed. Confess and repent as many times as necessary to throw him off and see yourself win the battle over this problem. Don't think that God won't forgive you again for the same thing you just confessed to Him last week. He forgives every time you confess sin before Him and fully repent of it.

Ask God every day to show you where your heart is not clean and right before Him. Don't let anything separate you from all He has for you.

Excess Baggage from the Past

Imagine that you are running in a race, and you're trying to reach the goal and win the prize. But as hard as you try you can never get to the finish line because there is a heavy weight tied around one of your legs. You struggle to pull it along, but it slows you down and causes you to be so exhausted that you want to give up. It doesn't occur to you that this is something you don't have to carry, yet you can't finish the race until you become free of it. That's what carrying around bad memories of past failures is like.

Many teenagers are hard on themselves about past failure. Or what they perceive as a failure on their part. They can become so discouraged about it that they feel like giving up and getting out of the race altogether. If you ever feel something similar yourself, remember that God wants to take away those bad memories so you will never have to carry them around with you again. (If it's a memory of something that someone did to you, I'll talk more about that in the next chapter.)

Whether it's something that happened a long time ago or as recently as yesterday, the past can keep you from moving into all God has for you. That's why He wants to set you free from it. And not only that, He wants to redeem and restore what has been lost or destroyed in your past and make it count for something important in your life now.

When you received Jesus, you became a new creation. He made all things new in your life. God wants you to forget the former things and reach forward to those things which are ahead (Philippians 3:13). He will help you do that. One of the great mysteries of the Lord is how He can take the horrible, the tragic, the painful, the devastating, and the embarrassing experiences and memories of our lives and not only heal them, but use them for good. It's not that He will make you unable to recall them, but He will heal you so thoroughly from their effects that you no longer think about them with any pain. He will give you a new life you will enjoy so much that you won't want to travel back in your mind to the old one.

The reason God doesn't want to wipe your past completely out of your memory is because He wants to use that part of your life for the work He has called you to do. He can take the worst thing about your past and make it to be your greatest blessing in the future. He will use you to bring hope to other people who have gone through a similar thing. He wants you to read your past like a history book, not like a prophecy for your future.

Tell God that you want to stay in the race. Tell Him you want to run in such a way so that you will obtain the prize (1 Corinthians 9:24).

Prayer Power

Lord, I realize that You know the secrets of my heart (Psalm 44:21). Reveal to me anything I am not seeing. Forgive me for any thoughts I have had, or words I have spoken, or things that I have done that are not pleasing to You. Specifically I confess to You (name anything you have done that you know is not pleasing to God). I confess it as sin and repent of it. Help me to make the changes I need to make.

I pray that You would set me free from my past. Help me to let go of any memory from my past that has kept me from moving into all You have for me. Specifically, I pray that You would set me free from (name any painful or bad memory you have). Everything that was done to me, or that I have done that causes me pain, I give to You. Thank You that You make all things new, and You are making me new in every way (Revelation 21:5). Release me from the past so I can move out of it and into the future You have for me. In Jesus' name I pray.

WORD POWER

If we confess our sins, He is faithful and just to forgive us our sins and to cleanse us from all unrighteousness.

1 JOHN 1:9

Beloved, if our heart does not condemn us, we have confidence toward God. And whatever we ask we receive from Him, because we keep His commandments and do those things that are pleasing in His sight.

1 JOHN 3:21-22

If anyone is in Christ, he is a new creation; old things have passed away; behold, all things have become new.

2 CORINTHIANS 5:17

1 When you read the Scriptures above, what do you think are the best reasons to confess and repent of your sins to God?

2 How do you feel after you confess and repent of your sins to God?

3 Write out a prayer telling God of any place you feel you are missing the mark in your life. Tell Him you want to be free of the torment of any past mistakes. If you find it hard to talk to God about these things, then ask Him to help you to communicate your heart to Him.

chapter 3

'LORD, HELP ME' Forgive Others

EVEN THOUGH MY MOTHER WAS ABUSIVE when I was growing up, my father wasn't. He was kind. When I became a Christian, forgiving my mother was the obvious thing to do, and that's what I did because I wanted to be free of the past. I didn't realize until years later that she wasn't the only one I needed to forgive.

I was talking to a friend one day who was a very strong believer, and I told her that I felt like my life wasn't going anywhere and I was very frustrated about it. She said she thought it was because I needed to forgive my dad. I told her she was wrong about that because my dad was the *good* parent.

"Just ask God about it," she said to me.

Later that day I did ask God about it, saying, "Lord, do I have any unforgiveness toward my dad?"

I expected God to assure me that I had nothing in my heart like that. But all of a sudden I realized that down deep I felt my dad never came through for me. He never rescued me from my mother's insanity. He never came and unlocked the closet so I could get out. I didn't realize how much I had blamed him for allowing my mother, who he knew was severely mentally ill, to treat me with such cruelty.

When I forgave my dad that day, I finally felt a sense of peace like I never had before. And after that there was real breakthrough in my life. I could feel my life moving in a good direction. I could sense God guiding me more than ever. When we don't forgive, it keeps us from moving on in our lives.

Most of the time we know when we haven't forgiven someone. We feel it in our heart. We don't want to forgive that person because what they did to us hurt a lot and we want them to pay for it in some way. And that ends up making us miserable.

I Prayed and God Answered
My relationship with my mother was on the rocks, so I prayed and now it is great.
(Age 16)

If you realize you haven't forgiven someone for something, confess it to God. And remember that *forgiving someone doesn't make them right; it makes you free.* In other words, when you forgive a person, it doesn't justify what they did. It's not saying that what they did wasn't wrong or hurtful. It's saying that you want to let go of it completely and move on with your life. If you don't, you will end up like I did, stuck right where you are and feeling that you are not getting anywhere.

Sometimes we can be unforgiving toward someone and not even recognize it. We *think* we are forgiving, but we really aren't. In order to make sure that doesn't happen to you, you need to do what I did and ask God to show you the truth about yourself. Say, "Lord, show me if there is anyone I have not forgiven." Then, when a person comes to mind who has said or done something hurtful to you, confess it to the Lord and ask Him to help you get free of it.

You will feel so good when you get that heavy weight of unforgiveness off your shoulders.

Making the Better Choice

I know "hate" is a very strong word, and we hate to use the word "hate" about anything. And we certainly hate the thought that we might actually have hate for another person. But that's what not forgiving is—the root of hate. When we entertain unforgiving thoughts, they turn to hate inside of us. And that can make us sick. It certainly makes us unattractive to others.

Jesus felt so strongly about this that He said, "Whoever hates his brother is a murderer, and you know that no murderer has eternal life abiding in him" (1 John 3:15). He also said,

The Hardest Thing About Prayer Is:

- When I feel like my prayers are hitting the ceiling
- When I can't hear God speaking to my heart
- When I don't know how to pray about something
- When I'm praying out loud in front of others
- When I don't feel like I'm connecting with God

(Ages 13-15)

"Whenever you stand praying, if you have anything against anyone, forgive him, that your Father in heaven may also forgive you your trespasses" (Mark 11:25).

Now let's get this straight. Jesus is saying that if we don't forgive someone, we are considered murderers without any eternal hope who shouldn't expect God to forgive us until we have forgiven others. I'd say that if it's between forgiving and not forgiving, forgiving seems like the better choice.

When we choose *not* to forgive, we end up walking in the dark (1 John 2:9-11). We can't see clearly, and so we stumble around in confusion. This throws our judgment off and we make mistakes. We become weak, sick, and bitter. Other people notice all this because our lack of forgiveness shows in our face, words, and actions. They see it even if they can't identify exactly what it is, and they don't feel comfortable around us.

When we choose to forgive, not only do *we* benefit, but so does everyone around us.

Putting Your Family First

It's extremely easy to have unforgiveness toward family members. That's because they are with us the most, know us the best, and can hurt us the deepest. But for those very same reasons, unforgiveness toward one of them will bring the greatest devastation to our lives. That's why forgiveness must start at home.

First of all, it is very important to make sure you have forgiven your mom and dad. The Bible is crystal clear about this. The fifth of the Ten Commandments says, "Honor your father and your mother, that your days may be long upon the land which the LORD your God is giving you" (Exodus 20:12). Not honoring your father and mother will make you miserable and shorten your life. And you can't fully honor them if you haven't forgiven them.

This is true no matter what your family situation is. It is true whether you have biological parents or adoptive parents. If one or both of your parents has died or moved away or abandoned you, you especially need to forgive them for doing that. I know of one girl who had to forgive her mom and dad for divorcing. I know of another who had to forgive her mother because her mother traveled a great deal in her work and left her daughter with her grandmother. The daughter knew her mother loved her, but she still had to forgive her for those times she felt abandoned because of her mother's absence.

My Prayer to God

Lord, this is my first time to ask for help. I have fallen into temptation and I need someone to believe in. If I don't have Your help, I know I will fall again and I don't want to do that. Please help me to be strong today.

(Age 17)

40

I know of a boy who had to forgive his dad for leaving his mom and his brothers and not coming back. He felt abandoned and thought his father didn't love him enough to stay. When the father later tried to reconcile with his son, he didn't want to have anything to do with his dad. He carried that hurt and didn't want to let it go. It wasn't until years later that the son was able to forgive the dad, and today they are very close. But many years were wasted carrying unforgiveness.

I know another boy who needed to forgive his mom because of the harsh and critical words she spoke to him practically every day. But he never forgave her and was miserable all his life because of it. My mom spoke cruelly to me too. She often told me that I was a worthless failure and would never amount to anything. It wasn't until I forgave her for all those words that I was able to stop thinking of myself as the failure she predicted and move into the success God had for me.

The Main Things I Pray About Are:
- Asking God's forgiveness
- Political issues
- That my school would be blessed by God
- My everyday problems
- My relationships (Ages 13-15)

When I made the decision to forgive my mother, I did it because I wanted to obey God. But forgiving her once did not mean that I never had to worry about forgiving her again. There were layers and layers of unforgiveness that had built up in me over the years, and I found I had to forgive her every time a bad memory of what she had done or said came to mind. Eventually I got free of everything.

Just because you confess your unforgiveness toward someone one day, it doesn't mean you won't have unforgiveness in you the next day for something else. That's why forgiveness is a choice you must make every day. You choose to forgive whether you feel like it or not. If you wait for good feelings toward that person to come first, you could end up waiting a lifetime. It's your responsibility to confess any unforgiveness to God and ask Him to help you forgive completely and move on with your life.

When You Feel You Can't Forgive

Forgiveness is never easy, but sometimes forgiveness can seem impossible in light of the devastating pain you have suffered. If you can think of someone you are having a hard time forgiving, ask God to help you. If someone has embarrassed you, rejected you, been rude to you, or said something bad about you to your face or behind your back, ask God to give you a heart of forgiveness for them. He will do that, even when it seems impossible. When you forgive someone, you release them into God's hands so *He* can deal with them. Forgiveness is actually the best revenge because it not only sets you free from the person you forgive, but it frees you to move into all the good things God has for you.

Remember that forgiving someone doesn't depend on that person admitting their guilt or apologizing to us. If it did, most of us would never be able to forgive anyone. We can forgive no matter what the other person does.

Sometimes we need to forgive *ourselves* for things we've done. Sometimes we need to forgive God when things have happened and we have blamed Him. Ask God to show you if you have either of these things in your heart. Don't let any kind of unforgiveness limit what God wants to do in your life.

Whatever It Takes

Four hundred and ninety times! That's how many times we have to forgive a person. Peter asked Jesus, "'Lord, how often shall my brother sin against me, and I forgive him? Up to seven times?' Jesus said to him, 'I do not say to you, up to seven times, but up to seventy times seven'" (Matthew 18:21-22).

God wants you to forgive as many times as it takes.

Jesus told a story of a man who was released from a *large* debt he owed his master. But then this man turned right around and made his own poor servant go to prison for not paying *him* a *small* debt. When the master heard about this, he said, "I forgave you that debt because you begged me. Shouldn't you have had compassion on your servant, just as I had compassion on you?"

I Feel Most Like Praying When:
- I am struggling with a tough situation
- My family or I have health problems
- I need wisdom
- I am sad or crying
- It's peaceful and quiet

(Ages 16-19)

The master was so angry that he delivered that man to the torturers until he paid back all of the debt.

Jesus said, "So My heavenly Father also will do to you if each of you, from his heart, does not forgive his brother his trespasses" (Matthew 18:35). This is very serious. We who have received Jesus have been forgiven a large debt. We have no right to be unforgiving of others. God says, "Be kind to one another, tender-hearted, forgiving one another, just as God in Christ forgave you" (Ephesians 4:32). If we don't forgive, we, too, will be imprisoned by our hatred and tortured by our bitterness.

Everything we do in life that lasts forever hinges on two things: loving God and loving others. It's far easier to love God than it is to love others, but God sees them as being the same. One of the most loving things we can do is forgive. It's hard to forgive those who have hurt, offended, or mistreated us. But God wants us to love even our enemies. And in the process of doing so, He perfects us (Matthew 5:48).

When you forgive others, it shows God how much you love Him. It opens your heart and mind and frees you to experience God's love in greater measure. It releases you to move in to all He has for you.

Prayer Power

Lord, help me to understand how much You have forgiven me so that I won't hold back forgiveness from others. Help me to forgive myself for the times I have failed. And if I have blamed You for things that have happened in my life, show me so I can confess it before You.

Help me to pray for those who hurt me so that my heart will be soft toward them. And if any person has unforgiveness toward me, show me what I can do to help resolve this issue between us. I pray You would soften their heart to forgive me.

Lord, show me if I have any unforgiveness toward my mother or father for anything they did or did not do. Help me to forgive any family member or friend every time I need to do so. I don't want anything to come between You and me, Lord. I don't want to limit what You want to do in my life because of my lack of forgiveness. In Jesus' name I pray.

WORD POWER

Judge not, and you shall not be judged. Condemn not, and you shall not be condemned. Forgive, and you will be forgiven.

LUKE 6:37

He who hates his brother is in darkness and walks in darkness, and does not know where he is going, because the darkness has blinded his eyes.

1 JOHN 2:11

If you forgive men their trespasses, your heavenly Father will also forgive you. But if you do not forgive men their trespasses, neither will your Father forgive your trespasses.

MATTHEW 6:14-15

1 Write out a prayer asking God to show you anyone you have not forgiven. If God shows you someone, ask Him to help you forgive him or her completely.

2 One of the ways you can more easily forgive someone is to pray for them. Write out a prayer for someone you need to forgive, no matter how long ago the offense against you occurred.

3 Write out a prayer asking God to show you if there is anyone who hasn't forgiven you for something. Ask Him to show you how to make things right between you.

chapter 4

'Lord, Help Me'

Do What's Right

WHEN I WAS IN HIGH SCHOOL IN CALIFORNIA, I had to take a required swimming class one semester. I hated it because it was at 7:30 every morning and my hair was wet and ruined for the rest of the day. We had to swim daily, rain or shine, and it could get very cold on those foggy California winter mornings. The only way I could be excused from swimming was if I were dying, and even then I had to have a note from a doctor.

In spite of the misery of that experience, I loved swimming and became good at it. I learned that if I was in the correct position and did all the right moves, just like my swimming instructor taught me, I could go forward quickly in the water. It became a smooth maneuver that would get me speedily to the other side of the giant pool. And nothing would make me falter—not even turbulence from other swimmers on either side of me.

The same principle is true for you and me. If we want to successfully navigate the waters of our lives, we must position ourselves correctly and learn all the right moves. If we don't, then when we come to turbulent situations we will not be able to navigate through them. We will end up flailing around and exhausting ourselves just trying to stay afloat. And we will never actually get anywhere. But when we position ourselves under the headship of Jesus and learn to do what He requires of us, there is a flow of the Holy Spirit that will carry us wherever we need to go.

All the Right Moves

The way we learn what God expects of us is by reading His Word. We can't begin to make the right moves if we don't know what they are. But that's just the beginning. We can study all we want and learn everything we are *supposed* to do, but we still have to *do* it. The swim instructor can tell us how to swim, but at some point we still have to jump in the water. It's one thing to make a list of dos and don'ts; it's quite another to have a heart for God's ways and a soul that longs to live them out. It's one thing to read about life; it's another to live it.

Obedience is something you do; having a heart to obey God and live His way is something you pray about. It's a lot easier to find out what we're *supposed* to be doing than it is to actually *do* it. That's why we need to pray that God will enable us to be disciplined enough to do what we need to do.

The Main Things I Pray About Are:

- For a thankful heart for all God has done for me
- For the safety and salvation of my school
- For my daily problems and concerns
- That I will have the courage to stand strong
- That I will daily praise God for who He is
(Ages 16-19)

I am a disciplined person, but I wasn't always that way. There was a time in my life when I was the exact opposite. Because I was plagued with depression, I couldn't think clearly or organize my life well. It's hard to do the things that are good for you when you don't know if you're worth it. It's hard to move forward in life when it takes all your energy just to survive each day.

When I started learning how to pray about everything, I asked God to help me be disciplined enough to read His Word and pray every day. I asked Him to help me understand how He wanted me to live and then help me to live that way. God answered those prayers. I now have become much more disciplined and organized. And I am obedient to God's ways beyond what I know I can do without His help. It didn't happen overnight. It happened a little at a time as I prayed about it and God answered my prayers.

I Believe in Prayer Because:

- I know that it works
- I have faith that God hears me
- I've seen other people's prayers answered
- It's the way we communicate with God
- It says in the Bible to pray

(Ages 16-19)

Don't get down on yourself if you don't do everything right. There is no one who can do that. That's why we need the Lord. Learning to live God's way takes a lifetime. There are always new things to learn, and we get into trouble when we think we know what to do and stop asking God if we're doing it. We can never get prideful about how perfectly we are obeying God because He is continually teaching us about His ways. And He will help us to live His way if we ask Him to. All you have to say is, "Lord, help me to obey You the way You want me to so I can become the person You created me to be." We should not "grow weary while doing good, for in due season we shall reap if we do not lose heart (Galatians 6:9).

The Things God Asks Us to Do Individually

In addition to the rules God wants everyone to obey, there are specific things He asks each one of us to do as individuals. He asks us to do these things in order to move us into the purpose He has for our lives. These are different for each person. For example, God might instruct you to learn a certain skill that He will not ask your friends to learn. He may ask you to take a certain class, work at a certain job, stop a certain activity, join a certain church, or change the way you've always done something. Whatever He asks you to do, remember He does this for your greatest blessing. It's important to pray, "Lord, show me what I am supposed to be doing." If you don't ask, you won't know.

Doing Things You'd Rather Not

We all have to do things we don't want to do. In even the most wonderful class or job, there are still things about it we don't enjoy. But part of being a success in life means that we do things even when we would rather not. When we do things we don't like simply because we know we need to do them, character is built in us. We become disciplined. We are formed into a leader God can trust. There is always a price to pay when we only do the things we *feel* like doing and don't do the things we *need* to do.

You have to make sacrifices for the good things you want. Whenever it's hard for you to do what you know you need to do, ask the Holy Spirit to help you. Of course, you still have to be the one to take the first step, no matter how much you don't want to. But when you do, the Holy Spirit will assist you the rest of the way.

I Pray for Others When:
- They have problems with their family
- They are in trouble
- They are unsaved
- They need encouragement
- They are hurting

(Ages 13-15)

Ten Good Reasons to Obey God

There are many reasons to obey God, but the best reason is because He said to. If there were no other reason, that would certainly be enough. Have you ever asked your parents why you had to do something and they said, "Because I said so"? What that means is they want you to do what they ask and trust that they know what's best. They are trying to teach you to be obedient to what they require of you. That's what God wants you to do too.

There are many more reasons to obey God that you should know about, and I have listed ten good ones below:

> **I Prayed and God Answered**
>
> I prayed I would stop being addicted to the Internet. Later, I found myself not really wanting to be on the Internet; it seemed boring. I felt like playing the piano and singing worship. It dawned on me later that it was an answer to prayer.
>
> (Age 13)

1. *When I obey God, He hears my prayers.* "If I regard iniquity in my heart, the Lord will not hear. But certainly God has heard me; He has attended to the voice of my prayer" (Psalm 66:18-19).

2. *When I obey God, I have a greater sense of His presence in my life.* "If anyone loves Me, he will keep My word; and My Father will love him, and We will come to him and make Our home with him" (John 14:23).

3. *When I obey God, I have greater wisdom.* "He stores up sound wisdom for the upright; He is a shield to those who walk uprightly" (Proverbs 2:7).

4. *When I obey God, I prove that I am His friend.* "You are My friends if you do whatever I command you" (John 15:14).

5. *When I obey God, I live in safety.* "You shall observe My statutes and keep My judgments, and perform them; and you will dwell in the land in safety" (Leviticus 25:18).

6. *When I obey God, I become a more loving person.* "Whoever keeps His word, truly the love of God is perfected in him" (1 John 2:5).

7. *When I obey God, good things happen to me.* "Behold, I set before you today a blessing and a curse: the blessing, if you obey the commandments of the LORD your God which I command you today" (Deuteronomy 11:26-27).

8. *When I obey God, I am happier.* "Happy is he who keeps the law" (Proverbs 29:18).

9. *When I obey God, I have peace.* "Mark the blameless man, and observe the upright; for the future of that man is peace" (Psalm 37:37).

10. *When I obey God, I will live longer.* "My son, do not forget my law, but let your heart keep my commands; for length of days and long life and peace they will add to you" (Proverbs 3:1-2).

Moving Into the Destiny God Has for You

God has great plans for you. He has important things He wants you to do. And He is preparing you for your destiny right now. But you have to take steps of obedience in order to get there. And you have to trust that He knows what's best and won't hurt you in the process. God doesn't have rules in order to make you miserable. God's rules are for *your* benefit. When you live by them, life works. When you don't live by them, life falls apart.

There is a definite connection between obedience and the love of God. Jesus said, "He who has My commandments and keeps them, it is he who loves Me. And he who loves Me will be loved by My Father, and I will love him and manifest Myself to him" (John 14:21). That means the way we show our love for God is living His way. And when we don't obey God, even though God loves us, we won't sense His love like we need to.

There is also a direct connection be-tween obedience and getting your prayers answered (1 John 3:22). If you have been frustrated because you don't see answers to your prayers, ask God if it is because of disobedience. Say, "Lord, is there any area of my life where I am not obeying You?" Don't keep telling God what *you* want without asking Him what *He* wants.

My Prayer to God
Lord, give me strength to stand up for You, even if others tease me. Give me the guts to stay strong, even if it seems impossible.
(Age 13)

God used that swimming class in my life in a way I couldn't have imagined. Because I remembered what my instructor taught me when I was learning how to swim, and I had practiced it diligently for years, it saved my life. One day I was at the beach with a friend and we were swimming in the ocean when a riptide took us out to sea. We couldn't get ourselves back to shore on our own, but we were able to swim with the tide and stay afloat until we were rescued by the lifeguards. If I hadn't obeyed my swim instructor years before and learned all the right moves, I hate to think what might have happened. Obeying God will save your life in more ways than one.

You never know when you will step into a special moment for which God has been preparing you. And it is not just one moment; He has many successive ones destined for your life. God is preparing you daily for something great. Something important. But you have to be attentive to your Instructor. "If anyone competes in athletics, he is not crowned unless he competes according to the rules" (2 Timothy 2:5). You can't swim into the mainstream of those moments successfully if you are not doing all the right moves now. But if you learn to do the right moves, you'll be ready for those special moments *and* whatever deep water you may find yourself in.

Prayer Power

Lord, Your Word says that those of us who love Your law will have great peace and nothing will cause us to stumble (Psalm 119:165). I love Your law because I know it is good and it's there for my benefit. Help me to obey You in every way so that I will not stumble and fall. If there are steps of obedience I need to take, open my eyes to see the truth and help me to take those steps. I know I can't do all things right without Your help, so I ask that You would help me to live in obedience to Your ways (Psalm 119:10).

Your Word says that "if we say we have no sin, we deceive ourselves, and the truth is not in us" (1 John 1:8). I don't want to deceive myself by not asking You where I am missing the mark You have set for my life. Reveal to me when I am not doing things I *should* be doing. Show me if I'm doing things I should *not* be doing. Help me to hear Your specific instructions to me. Speak to me clearly through Your Word so I will understand what's right and what's wrong. I don't want to grieve the Holy Spirit in anything I do (Ephesians 4:30). Help me to always be learning about Your ways so I can live in the fullness of Your presence and move into all You have for me. In Jesus' name I pray.

WORD POWER

Whatever we ask we receive from Him, because we keep His commandments and do those things that are pleasing in His sight.

1 JOHN 3:22

For the LORD God is a sun and shield; the LORD will give grace and glory; no good thing will He withhold from those who walk uprightly.

PSALM 84:11

Blessed are those who hear the word of God and keep it!

LUKE 11:28

1

The law of God that I have the most difficult time obeying is:

Write out a prayer asking God to help you obey Him in this area.

2

Of the "Ten Good Reasons to Obey God" on pages 51-52 which three are the most important to you in terms of inspiring you to obey God's laws?

3

The area of my life where I would like to have more discipline is:

Write out a prayer asking God to help you be more disciplined in that area of obedience.

chapter 5

Lord, Help Me
Stand Strong Against Bad Influences

THERE ISN'T A PLACE ON EARTH WHERE YOU can be absolutely sure there are no bad influences. That's because evil can be anywhere. Sometimes it seems like it's everywhere. So you're going to be faced with bad influences at some point in your life. You probably already have, to some extent, and the earlier you learn to recognize them, the better.

The thing you need to know is that anyone who has given their life to God is a *target* for evil influences. That's because you have an enemy. Anyone who loves God and stands for the things God stands for has an enemy. That enemy opposes all that God is, everything He does, and anyone who believes in Him. The enemy will try to ruin your life. You have to be ready for him.

Your enemy is the devil. He was created by God for good, but he became prideful and chose to rebel against God. He wanted to *be* God and have all created beings worship him. Because of that he fell from God's presence in heaven to the earth, where he never gets tired of looking for someone to destroy.

The good news is that we who know the Lord have power over him. Our enemy is not all-knowing, and he is not always present. He is not able to be everywhere, and he cannot know our every thought. But if we don't fully realize that he is already a *defeated* enemy, then we can be harassed by him continually. He can use other people who don't know God to try and influence us away from the life God has for us.

One of the things Jesus accomplished when He died on the cross and rose again was to break the power of the enemy over our lives. He gave believers authority over him, saying, "I give you the authority…over all the power of the enemy, and nothing shall by any means hurt you" (Luke 10:19).

We are all involved in an ongoing spiritual battle with an enemy who will never let up. The Bible tells us that "we do not wrestle against flesh and blood, but against principalities, against powers, against the rulers of the darkness of this age, against spiritual hosts of wickedness in the heavenly places" (Ephesians 6:12). Even when we are being treated badly or influenced to do wrong by a particular person, we still have to recognize who our *real* enemy is. This will be our first step in standing strong against him and the people he influences who will try to influence *you*.

Just as God has a plan for your

The Hardest Thing About Prayer Is:

- Staying still for that long
- Knowing what to pray about
- Being worried that it won't work
- Not knowing if God is listening
- Being truthful and honest

(Ages 13-15)

life, so does Satan. Satan's plan is to destroy you. "The thief does not come except to steal, and to kill, and to destroy" (John 10:10). Satan never takes a day off, so he is constantly trying to see his plan for your life fulfilled. That's why you have to watch out for bad influences. The Bible says you have to "be sober, be vigilant; because your adversary the devil walks about like a roaring lion, seeking whom he may devour" (1 Peter 5:8).

I Feel Most Like Praying When:
- I am afraid
- I feel guilty
- After I have read the Bible
- I am alone
- All the time

(Ages 16-19)

Most of the time you can recognize an obvious attack of the enemy against you. For example, if someone offers you alcohol or an illegal drug, you know it's wrong. You have to say no immediately and get away from that person. Drugs and alcohol destroy the mind and soul as well as the body. Ask anyone who is dying from a disease caused by drugs and alcohol if they regret having gotten hooked. They will tell you that they deeply regret falling for the deception of thinking, *It won't hurt if I just have a little.* This is a lie of the enemy designed for our destruction, because addictions happen one step at a time until the person is addicted and can't stop. Getting you hooked on drugs and alcohol is part of the enemy's plan for your destruction.

Pornography is another bad influence that is obvious. Most people know pornography is wrong the moment they accidentally see it, and they immediately turn their eyes away from it. But some people think that it doesn't hurt anyone to look at it. The truth is, it hurts the person who sees it more than they realize. It plants a hook on the inside of them that will draw them to it more and more. It's addictive and will eventually destroy that person's life. Pornography is another part of the enemy's plan to destroy you.

Driving Under His Influence

Before I became a believer, I got into drugs and alcohol to try to get rid of the pain and depression I felt all the time. I thought they would help, but they didn't. Although they *seemed* to help temporarily, afterward I felt worse than ever about myself and my life. I became careless and almost killed myself a number of times. Once when I nearly overdosed, I pleaded with a God I didn't even know that if He would save me from death I wouldn't take drugs again. He kept His part of the bargain, but I wasn't able to keep mine.

One time when I drove under the influence of drugs, I almost had a head-on collision. I was driving myself to the airport to catch a very early flight and didn't realize that the drugs I had taken the night before were still affecting me. I was thinking that I had taken them on a different day so it was okay, but actually it was only a few hours earlier. I was driving fast because I had overslept and was very late, which was a big mistake in the first place. As I came up over a hill, an ambulance was coming full speed in the opposite direction headed straight for me. I didn't see it or hear the siren screaming until it was practically on top of me. The ambulance swerved to the left and I swerved to the right and we missed hitting head-on by a fraction of an inch. There was so little air between our vehicles that it shook my car violently. I knew I had just missed death or severe debilitation.

That incident shook me up in many ways. It scared me that I was under the influence of those drugs

The Main Things I Pray About Are:

- That I know God's will for my life
- That I get along with my stepmom
- That my dad will be saved
- That I will be protected from evil
- That my family and I will be healthy

(Ages 13-15)

and didn't even realize it. That I was so out of it I didn't even hear the siren. I knew if I didn't change my ways it was going to be all over for me. What had started out a couple years earlier as just trying something offered to me at a social gathering became something that nearly destroyed my life. I had come under a bad influence and wasn't strong enough to stop it until I found the Lord.

There are many bad influences around, some blatant and others not so obvious. The subtle ones can seduce you into receiving something bad into your life without you even realizing it.

I Prayed and God Answered

When my grandpa had a heart attack, he only had a 25 percent chance of living. My cousins and I prayed and prayed. The surgery was successful and he lived. I am so grateful because he is a godly man and a big influence on my life.
(Age 13)

Something that will ultimately get you off the path God has for you and destroy your life. An example of that is sexual promiscuity. So much of it is portrayed on television and in the movies that it's easy to get used to the idea of it to the point that it doesn't seem like a big deal anymore. It appears that "everybody is doing it." But that is not true. It *is* a big deal. And not everyone is doing it.

The problem with sexual activity outside of marriage is that it can happen in a moment of weakness if you are not careful. You have to be cautious in your relationships with others and not allow them to cross the line of what is right in God's sight in even the slightest way. God designed sex to be kept for the person He has for you to marry. When a person has sex outside of God's will for their lives, it brings destruction to the inner person. It limits what God wants to do in you.

In order to avoid these and other kinds of bad influences, you need to come under the influence of the Lord. Pray that God will help you discern the influences around you. If you stay close to

God and in His Word, He will reveal the enemy's work in your life. He will show you where you are in dangerous territory. He will give you discernment when you are being set up and help you see the truth.

If you have already come under a bad influence, God will give you the power to put a stop to it. He promises that you can "resist the devil and he will flee from you" (James 4:7).

Five Weapons to Use Against the Enemy

God has given us many weapons to use against the enemy. Here are the top five:

1. *A powerful weapon against the enemy is God's Word.* Jesus Himself used this weapon against the devil when He was led into the wilderness by the Holy Spirit and Satan came to tempt Him (Matthew 4:1). One would think that if you were the Son of God you wouldn't have to go into the wilderness at all, let alone to be tempted by the devil. But "the tempter came to Him" (verse 3) the way he comes to all of us, and Jesus used the Word of God to refute him. He said, "Man shall not live by bread alone, but by every word that proceeds from the mouth of God" (verse 4).

   When the devil tries to influence your life in any way, speak the Word like Jesus did. The moment you sense that you are being swayed by bad influences, run to the Word of God and begin quoting it. Say, "I can do all things through Christ who strengthens me" (Philippians 4:13). The devil hates that and will leave you alone.

2. *A powerful weapon against the enemy is praise.* The devil also hates it every time we worship God. That's because he can't tolerate people worshiping anyone else but *him.* He detests it so much he can't even be around it. When we praise and

worship the Lord, God's presence dwells powerfully in our midst and the devil has to leave.

3. *A powerful weapon against the enemy is obedience.* If we are living in sin or walking in disobedience in any way, this leaves the door open in our lives for the devil to gain a point of entry and ultimately a foothold. Bad things happen when our own *ongoing* sin gives the enemy an invitation to erect a stronghold in our life. Satan does not have jurisdiction over you, but disobedience to the laws of God puts out a welcome mat for him. You can shut the door in his face by confessing your mistakes and repenting of them before the Lord.

4. *A powerful weapon against the enemy is faith.* Keep in mind that the enemy is always planting land mines out ahead of you. You have no idea where they are because they are not visible to the human eye. The way to avoid them is to walk close with God and let Him guide your steps. God says about the enemy that we are to "resist him, steadfast in the faith, knowing that the same sufferings are experienced by your brotherhood in the world" (1 Peter 5:9). That means we put our faith in God and refuse to do what the enemy wants. Walking under God's influence through faith in God's Word is a powerful way to avoid the enemy's trap.

5. *A powerful weapon against the enemy is prayer.* The enemy detests it when we talk to God. That's because even *he* knows that God hears our prayers and answers. The enemy will try to get us to doubt that God hears us at all so he can weaken us. But don't fall for that lie. Say, "Lord, help me to resist the enemy and the evil influences he brings into my life," and then take comfort in knowing that this simple prayer has enough power to break the back of the enemy.

If I'm a Good Person, Why Am I Being Attacked?

Why are good people attacked? The answer is in the question itself. The enemy attacks you because you *are* a good person. The devil wants to destroy anyone he can, but he especially wants to destroy anyone who loves God and lives His way. In fact, this is the main reason he is your enemy. The only way you could get him to not do that is to become like him. You would have to stand for what *he* represents.

Keep in mind that the greater your commitment is to the Lord, the more the devil will try to harass you. He will do all he can to wear you down with confusion, discouragement, guilt, fear, depression, temptation, or defeat. Even though he is not close to being as powerful as God, he will try to make you think that he is. He will attempt to gain a place of entry and rule in your life by deceiving you. He will try to blind you to the truth and get you to follow a path that is not the way of the Lord for you. Don't believe his lies. He will try to convince you he is winning the battle, but the truth is that he has already lost. He lost the moment you surrendered your life to the Lord.

Surrendering Your Life to the One Who Loves You Most

Let there be no doubt; no one loves you more than God. Because He loves you, He has your best interests in mind all the time, but He wants you to surrender your life to *Him* and not to anyone or anything else. The truth is, you can't move into all God has for you until you do. This means being willing to say, "Lord, whatever You want me to do, I'll do it. I will say yes to anything You ask of me. I will do whatever You say so that I can please You and move into all You have for me."

This attitude of surrender means putting God first and submitting to Him. And it makes all the difference. When we personally declare Jesus to be Lord over our life, it shows we are controlled by the Spirit and not the flesh. "No one can say that Jesus is Lord except by the Holy Spirit" (1 Corinthians 12:3). When we are controlled by the Spirit and not the flesh, it is a lot easier to resist the enemy.

Why do we sometimes find it hard to say, "Whatever You want, Lord. I'll do anything You ask"? It's because we want what we want, and we're afraid God might ask us to give up something we want. We think He might ask us to do something that won't be for our greatest good. But that's wrong. When we let God rule our life, He will do great things through us and give us more than we ever dreamed possible. Ask God to help you give Him what *He* wants so that you will never give the enemy what he wants.

My Prayer to God
Lord, I thank You for today. Give me direction concerning alcohol, drugs, and sexual matters. The things of this world are so hard to overcome. Help my friends at school with this too.
(Age 13)

Prayer Power

Lord, I thank You for dying on the cross for me and rising again to defeat my enemy. Thank You that You have given me all authority over him (Luke 10:19). Thank You that by the power of Your Holy Spirit I can successfully resist the devil and he has to leave me alone (James 4:7).

The way I feel that the enemy is trying hardest to influence my life is (name any place where you feel the pull of a bad influence). Help me to be strong to resist that pull. Show me what to do to avoid it. If I need to talk with someone about it, show me who I can trust to listen confidentially and give me sound advice. I surrender myself and my life to You and invite You to rule in my mind, soul, body, and spirit. I declare You to be Lord over every area of my life. Help me to move in the

Spirit and not the flesh so that I can always walk away from evil influences and not toward them.

Lord, I know that I don't have to be afraid of the enemy (Deuteronomy 20:3). Thank You that even though the enemy tries to influence me to do his will, You have given me the power to escape him completely (2 Timothy 2:26). Thank You that You have set me free from him (Psalm 18:17). Thank You that I will never be brought down by the enemy as long as I stand strong in You. In Jesus' name I pray.

WORD POWER

The Lord is faithful, who will establish you and guard you from the evil one.

2 THESSALONIANS 3:3

The righteous cry out, and the LORD hears, and delivers them out of all their troubles.

PSALM 34:17

Take up the whole armor of God, that you may be able to withstand in the evil day, and having done all, to stand. Stand therefore, having girded your waist with truth, having put on the breastplate of righteousness, and having shod your feet with the preparation of the gospel of peace; above all, taking the shield of faith with which you will be able to quench all the fiery darts of the wicked one. And take the helmet of salvation, and the sword of the Spirit, which is the word of God; praying always with all prayer and supplication in the Spirit, being watchful to this end with all perseverance and supplication for all the saints.

EPHESIANS 6:13-18

1

What most concerns you about the bad influences you see in the world around you? How can you avoid them?

2

What bad influences do you think you are most susceptible to at this time and place in your life? Write out a prayer asking God to help you be especially strong in that area. (For example, "Lord, I don't ever want to stumble into any kind of bad thing on the Internet. Help me to always recognize places and people that are not good and be able to resist going where they are.")

3

If you have ever fallen into a trap of the enemy, write out a prayer asking God to set you completely free from it. If nothing like that has ever happened to you, write out a prayer asking God to keep you under *His* influence and away from bad influences.

chapter 6

'LORD, HELP ME'

Take Control of My Mind

Do you ever have thoughts in your mind that are upsetting to you but you can't seem to get rid of them? Do you ever have thoughts that make you feel sad or lonely? Or depressed or anxious? Or discouraged? Have you ever felt so bad about yourself and your life that you didn't want to go anywhere or see anyone? I have had those kinds of thoughts too.

Many people think thoughts like that *sometimes*. Some people think thoughts like that *a lot of the time*. The enemy wants us to think bad thoughts *all of the time*. But God doesn't want us to think that way *at all*.

I used to think that every thought that came into my mind was real. If I was depressed it meant I had to live with that emotion. It was just the way I was and I could do nothing to change it. But I was so wrong. I was believing a lie.

Sometimes the thoughts you have are for a very good reason. There is definitely something you can point to that is making you think and feel that way. But too often you can have negative emotions and you don't even know why. There may be nothing really wrong with you or your life, and so you wonder why you can't get on top of them. When that happens you can be certain the enemy is trying to get you to believe a lie.

Learning to Take Control

Do you realize you don't have to allow certain thoughts into your mind at all? It's true. You have control over that. A big part of standing strong against the enemy is taking control over our minds. The Bible says that we must learn to bring "every thought into captivity" (2 Corinthians 10:5). It was an astounding revelation to me when I became a new believer and learned that I didn't have to entertain every thought that came into my head. I had a choice about whether to listen to my thoughts or not. Isn't that amazing?

Many criminals talk about how they heard a voice in their head telling them to commit a crime and they just followed orders. When people are not taught to discern the voices in their head, they don't recognize the voice of the enemy. He is a clever deceiver who will come to each one of us and try to speak lies into our mind. We have to be ready for him by being able to identify and resist his lies. We have to catch his lies the minute they enter our mind so that we don't entertain them as truth and make ourselves miserable.

One of the most difficult things about being a teenager is that you are such a passionate thinker. You feel

I Pray for Others When:
- They need a miracle
- I see them in the school halls
- They are in trouble for doing wrong
- They feel hopeless
- I want to invite them to church

(Ages 16-19)

things strongly. This is a good trait, but at this period in your life it can cause your emotions to go from one extreme to another in a short period of time. Extremely happy or excited one minute; extremely sad or depressed the next. Extremely anxious or worried one day; extremely carefree and unconcerned the next.

You may also feel you cannot express your thoughts and feelings to the depth that you would like. You might be embarrassed to have anyone know you are feeling the way you do. In fact, your thoughts and feelings may be so complex that you don't even know how to talk about them. You are not sure you completely understand them yourself. And so they build up and become like a volcano that is ready to erupt. (More about that in chapter 13.) The enemy would like to step into that situation and take advantage of your passion. He would like you to lose your temper or get so depressed that you do something hurtful to someone or yourself. This wonderful passion of yours, that should be used for God's glory, can be turned into a weapon against you by the enemy in a moment if he can get you to believe his lies.

> **I Think of God As:**
> • An Advisor
> • An Answer
> • A Comforter
> • My Healer
> • My Helper
> (Ages 16-19)

The Lies We Believe

Do you ever have certain thoughts that play over and over in your mind like an old broken record? Have you ever had a thought that produces a physical feeling in your body, such as a pain in your heart, a queasy sensation in the pit of your stomach, tightness in your throat, weakness in your arms and legs, a fear or a dread, a nervousness or anxiety, tears in your eyes, a rash on your face and neck, or a rapidly beating heart?

Do you ever have any "what if " thoughts plague your mind, such as "What if I jumped off the balcony?" "What if I ran my car into that wall?" "What if my parents die?" "What if I can't be successful?"

Have you ever had "if only" thoughts that make you miserable? Such as "If only I hadn't done that." "If only I had been there, this wouldn't have happened." "If only I wouldn't have said those words to that person."

Do you ever have self-punishing thoughts? Such as "No one cares about me." "I'm such a failure." "I'm no good." "Nothing I do turns out right." "I'm not attractive."

If you've had thoughts like any of these mentioned above, please know that this is not God speaking into your life. This is the enemy of your soul trying to gain control of your mind.

Difficult times do happen, but too often we suffer unnecessarily because of lies we believe about ourselves and our situations. We accept as fact the words that are spoken by an enemy who wants us destroyed. We can become fearful, depressed, lonely, angry, doubtful, confused, insecure, hopeless, beaten down, worried, and discouraged all because of lies we believe. The good news is that we can overcome each one of these lies with prayer, the truth of God's Word, and with praise to God.

The Main Things I Pray About Are:

- For wisdom
- To stay strong
- For help
- My pets
- My friends

(Ages 13-15)

Be aware that one of the enemy's tactics is to try and steal God's Word from you. He will do that by first of all getting you to *question God's Word*, just like he did with Eve in the Garden of Eden. He will say things like "Did God really say that?" "Will God really mind if you do that?" He will *contradict God's Word* and get you to think things like "God doesn't really mean that."

The enemy will also try to get you to doubt God's love for you. "God doesn't think you're anything special." "If God really loved you, He wouldn't withhold anything good from you." Whenever the thoughts you have begin to question and contradict God's Word, you can know for sure that you are being set up by the enemy. Remember, "there is a way that seems right to a man, but its end is the way of death" (Proverbs 14:12). Certain thoughts may appear to you to be accurate, but when you hold them up next to God's Word, the lie is exposed.

Deception is the enemy's ongoing plan of attack. Jesus said the devil "was a murderer from the beginning, and does not stand in the truth, because there is no truth in him. When he speaks a lie, he speaks from his own resources, for he is a liar and the father of it" (John 8:44). The only power the devil has over you is getting you to believe his lies. If you don't believe his lies, he is powerless to do anything in your life.

I Prayed and God Answered

I prayed for courage to go out and make friends and not keep to myself. Now God has given me great friends that are strong in the Lord and I can be honest and open about God with them.

(Age 16)

Choose Your Thoughts Carefully

Just as you can turn the television on and off, you have a choice about what you will or will not accept into your mind. You can choose to take every thought captive like the Bible says to do (2 Corinthians 10:5) and "let this mind be in you which was also in Christ Jesus" (Philippians 2:5) or you can allow the devil to feed you lies and manipulate your life.

Every sin begins as a thought in the mind. "For from within, out of the heart of men, proceed evil thoughts, adulteries, fornications, murders, thefts, covetousness, wickedness, deceit, lewdness, an evil eye, blasphemy, pride, foolishness" (Mark 7:21-22).

The truth is, if you don't take control of your mind, the devil will. That's why you must be diligent to monitor what you allow into your mind. What TV shows, magazines, and books do you look at? What music, radio programs, or CDs do you listen to? Do they fill your mind with godly thoughts and feed your spirit so you feel happy, clear-minded, peaceful, and good about yourself and your life, or do they deplete you and leave you feeling empty, confused, anxious, fearful, and bad about yourself and your life? "God is not the author of confusion but of peace" (1 Corinthians 14:33). When we fill our minds with God's Word and books and magazines and music glorifying to God, we leave no room for the enemy's propaganda.

If you want to know whether your thoughts are from the enemy or the Lord, ask yourself, "Are these thoughts I would *choose* to have? Do I *want* to think this way?" If you answer no, then they are probably from your enemy. If, for example, you are sitting in school or church and you suddenly have impure thoughts about someone, rather than beat yourself up for that, tell the enemy to get off your brain. Tell him you refuse to be a dumping ground for his trash. Tell him you "have the mind of Christ" and you won't listen to anything that is inconsistent with that (1 Corinthians 2:16).

Refusing to entertain bad or depressing thoughts is part of doing our job to resist the devil. How many people have we known or heard about who should have done that and didn't? The Bible says that you are supposed to stop your old ways of doing things, "be renewed in the spirit of your mind," and let God give you a new way to think that is true and right (Ephesians 4:22-24).

You don't have to live with confusion or mental oppression. You don't have to listen to a voice telling you to do something you know you shouldn't. You don't have to "walk as the rest of the Gentiles walk, in the futility of their mind, having their understanding darkened, being alienated from the life of God, because of the ignorance that is in them, because of the hardening of their heart" (Ephesians 4:17-18). You can have clarity and knowledge and truth. You can choose to have positive thoughts and not negative ones.

My Prayer to God
Lord, sometimes I feel like no one out there even cares, so I ask You to comfort me and show me that someone does.
(Age 14)

If ever your enemy tries to convince you that your future is as hopeless as his, or that you are a failure with no purpose, value, gifts, or abilities, know that God says exactly the opposite. Reading what He says in His Word is the first step toward taking control of your mind. For example, when a thought comes into your mind that says, "God doesn't care about you enough to answer your prayers," you can immediately identify that as a lie from the pit. God says in His Word, "If you abide in Me, and My words abide in you, you will ask what you desire, and it shall be done for you" (John 15:7). If you fill your mind with what God says, you'll never fall for a counterfeit.

Prayer Power

Lord, show me any place in my mind where I have accepted a lie as the truth. I don't want to think futile and foolish thoughts or give place to thoughts that are not glorifying to You (Romans 1:21). I don't want to walk according to my own thinking (Isaiah 65:2). I want to bring every thought captive so I can control my mind.

Your Word is "a discerner of the thoughts and intents of the heart" (Hebrews 4:12). As I read Your Word, speak to my heart about any wrong thinking in me. May Your Word be so etched in my mind that I will be able to identify a lie of the enemy the minute I hear it. Spirit of Truth, keep me undeceived. I know You have given me authority "over all the power of the enemy" (Luke 10:19), and so I refuse to listen to lies.

I refuse to have confusion in my mind because You, Lord, give me clarity of thought.

Thank You that I "have the mind of Christ" (1 Corinthians 2:16). I want Your thoughts to be my thoughts. Show me where I have filled my mind with anything that is ungodly. Show me when I allow thoughts into my mind through television, the Internet, books, magazines, films, or music that are not of You. Help me to resist doing that and instead fill my mind with thoughts, words, music, and images that are glorifying to You. Help me to think upon what is true, noble, just, pure, lovely, of good report, virtuous, and praiseworthy (Philippians 4:8). I lay claim to the "sound mind" that You have given me (2 Timothy 1:7). In Jesus' name I pray.

WORD POWER

Do not be conformed to this world, but be transformed by the renewing of your mind, that you may prove what is that good and acceptable and perfect will of God.

ROMANS 12:2

Though we walk in the flesh, we do not war according to the flesh. For the weapons of our warfare are not carnal but mighty in God for pulling down strongholds, casting down arguments and every high thing that exalts itself against the knowledge of God, bringing every thought into captivity to the obedience of Christ.

2 CORINTHIANS 10:3-5

You will keep him in perfect peace, whose mind is stayed on You, because he trusts in You.

ISAIAH 26:3

1. Can you identify any negative or confusing thoughts you have that you would like to get rid of? Write out a prayer to God asking Him to help you take control of your mind and get rid of them.

2. Some of the thoughts I have had in the past that were probably from the enemy and not of the Lord are:

3. Write out a prayer telling God of any thoughts you have now or have had in the recent past that are troubling and upsetting for you and you know they are destructive for your life. (For example, say, "Lord, I have been struggling with thoughts about dying and this is making me sad." Or "I have unreasonable thoughts of failing.")

chapter 7

'LORD, HELP ME'

Understand Your Word

YOUR MIND AND BODY NEED FOOD EVERY DAY. Did you know that your spirit and soul need food every day too? The kind of food that feeds your spirit and soul is God's Word. Just as your mind and body don't get fed if you don't eat, your spirit and soul don't get fed if you don't read God's Word. You can't live successfully without food for your spirit and soul.

Before I became a believer, there were a few times I had read passages in the Bible, but I couldn't understand them very well. They didn't come alive to me. After I received the Lord, it was a different story. Because I now had the Holy Spirit in me teaching me as I read, I could understand more and more every time I read God's Word. I could sense my spirit getting lighter and my mind becoming clearer. Every time I read anything in the Bible, I felt that I knew God better and my faith in Him was growing stronger. When I felt sad, fearful, anxious, or depressed, I would read the Bible and those feelings would lift and be replaced with peace, hope, and joy. I soon realized that I could not get through a day without reading something in God's Word.

The Hardest Thing About Prayer Is:

- Making myself just do it
- Being patient for the answers
- Admitting what I really need
- Being consistent to pray every day
- Everything about it is hard

(Ages 16-19)

If God's Word is food for our souls, then we can't live without it. Jesus quoted God's Word, saying, "Man shall not live by bread alone, but by every word that proceeds from the mouth of God" (Matthew 4:4). That means that just eating food will never be enough for us because we will always be empty unless we are spiritually fed too. If we are not continually fed with God's Word, we will starve and waste away spiritually.

You'll be amazed at how much difference it will make in your life if you read God's Word every day. You don't have to read a lot, just something. Anything is better than nothing. That's why it is important to pray that God will help you to find the time to do it and enable you to understand it. And you have to pray that His Word will *stay* in your heart so that you don't forget it and lose the full benefit of it. The Bible says that "we must give the more earnest heed to the things we have heard, lest we drift away" (Hebrews 2:1). We don't realize how quickly we forget.

Doing the Word

Every time you read the Bible, you learn something new, even if it is a passage you have read a hundred times before. It doesn't matter how long you walk with God; He always has something new for you to learn in His Word. It may be new dimensions of what you already know, or it may be something you have never seen before. Either way, it's not enough to just learn the truth; you must act on it too. God says to "be doers of the word, and not hearers only, deceiving yourselves. For if anyone is a hearer of the word and not a doer, he is like a man observing his natural face in a mirror; for he observes himself, goes away, and immediately forgets what kind of man he was" (James 1:22-24).

That means if we just read the Word and don't do what it says, we not only forget what it says, but we also forget who we are in the Lord. James goes on to say that when we do what God's Word says, we will be blessed in everything we do (James 1:25). That's a great promise. Whenever you read God's Word, ask Him to help you apply it to your life and do what it says. Then take a step that shows you understand and believe what you read and are going to live like it.

It's possible to *hear* the Word, *read* the Word, and even *teach* the Word and still remain unchanged and unaffected by it. We don't want that to happen to us. All Scripture will teach us, convict us, enrich us, heal us, warn us, and expose our hearts, but we have to act on it. That's why you need to ask God to speak to your heart every time you read His Word and show you what you should be doing in response to it.

I Feel Most Like Praying When:

- I feel lost or confused
- I get up in the morning
- I am in bed in the dark
- I need a lift
- I feel down, sad, or upset

(Ages 16-19)

Ten Reasons to Read God's Word

A lot of people have trouble reading God's Word as often as they need to. If you are one of those people, check out the following ten reasons to read the Bible. I know they will inspire you.

1. *I read God's Word so that I will know where I am going in life.* You can't see the future or know *exactly* where you are heading, but God's Word will guide you. It will keep you on the right path. It puts a holy compass in your heart and helps you stay on the path God has for you. "Direct my steps by Your word, and let no iniquity have dominion over me" (Psalm 119:133).

2. *I read God's Word so that I can have wisdom.* Nothing is more important than having wisdom because it will direct you and keep you from making big mistakes. Knowledge of God's Word is where wisdom begins to grow in you. "The law of the LORD is perfect, converting the soul; the testimony of the LORD is sure, making wise the simple" (Psalm 19:7).

3. *I read God's Word so that I can find success in my life.* When you live according to the teachings of the Bible, life works and things turn out well. "This Book of the Law shall not depart from your mouth, but you shall meditate in it day and night, that you may observe to do according to all that is written in it. For then you will make your way prosperous, and then you will have good success" (Joshua 1:8).

4. *I read God's Word so that I can be cleansed and prepared for the Lord's presence.* You don't want to go through life without a sense of the Lord's presence guiding and helping you. God wants you to be cleansed of everything that is impure in order to enjoy more of His presence. One of the ways you are made pure is through reading His Word. It washes your spirit and soul. "How can a young man cleanse his way? By taking heed according to Your word" (Psalm 119:9).

5. *I read God's Word so that I can obey Him.* If you don't understand what God's laws are, how can you obey them? And you want to live God's way because that's when things work out.

"Teach me, O LORD, the way of Your statutes, and I shall keep it to the end. Give me understanding, and I shall keep Your law; indeed, I shall observe it with my whole heart. Make me walk in the path of Your commandments, for I delight in it" (Psalm 119:33-35).

6. *I read God's Word so that I can have joy.* Joy is something you can have no matter what is happening in your life. You can't live well without it. You can't be free of anxiety and unrest without the Word of God in your heart. "The statutes of the LORD are right, rejoicing the heart; the commandment of the LORD is pure, enlightening the eyes" (Psalm 19:8).

7. *I read God's Word so that I can have more faith.* Faith in God's Word is what makes it active in your life. Faith makes things happen the way they need to happen. You can't grow in faith without reading and hearing the Word of God. "So then faith comes by hearing, and hearing by the word of God" (Romans 10:17).

8. *I read God's Word so that I can be delivered from things that hold me back from moving into all God has for me.* You won't always know what you need to be free of unless you study God's Word to find out. "If you abide in My word, you are My disciples indeed. And you shall know the truth, and the truth shall make you free" (John 8:31-32).

9. *I read God's Word so that I can have peace.* Everybody needs peace in their lives. Peace gives you strength to face each day, knowing everything will be all right. God's peace is greater than any kind of peace the world offers, but you must find it first in His Word. "Great peace have those who love Your law, and nothing causes them to stumble" (Psalm 119:165).

10. *I read God's Word so that I can tell the difference between good and evil.* People today are teaching that evil things are good

and good things are evil. It is becoming more and more difficult to know for sure what is right and wrong. Only God's Word will tell you clearly. "Your word I have hidden in my heart, that I might not sin against You" (Psalm **119:11**).

Going for the Gold

God has gold and diamonds everywhere in His Word, but we must dig them out. And just like all precious gems and metals when they are first pulled out of the ground, the treasures you find in God's Word need to be polished and refined in us in order to have the beauty and brilliance they are capable of revealing. Every time you go over one of God's promises in your heart, it will become more refined and polished in you and shine more brightly in your soul.

I Prayed and God Answered

I prayed for three years to be able to buy my favorite horse. He wasn't for sale. Now I have had that horse for two years and he means a lot to me.

(Age 15)

One of the most priceless gems you will find in the Word is God's *voice*. He speaks to us through His Word as we read it or hear it. In fact, we can't really learn to recognize God's voice to our soul if we are not hearing Him speak to us first in His Word. The more you hear His voice in the Word, the easier it will be to recognize Him speaking to your heart when you are out in the world. The more you can discern God's voice, the less chance there will be that you will accept any kind of counterfeit.

God's Word straightens out our mind and soul and helps us to think clearly about things. It leads us away from self-destructive thoughts and enables us to enjoy a sense of well-being. It gives us hope and keeps us on course. It provides us with a solid foundation upon which to build a life of success and peace. God looks forward to meeting you in His Word every day, and He wants you to feel the same way.

There is no way to draw close to God or have a clean and right heart or be a forgiving person or do what's right or stand against the enemy or take control of your mind unless you are in the Word of God every day. Even if it's only a verse or two that you read. Or take a verse and say it over and over to get it into your mind and your heart. For example, if you were to take the verse "I can do all things through Christ who strengthens me" (Philippians 4:13) and say it over and over throughout the day, it will powerfully affect your life that day. God's Word is your compass and your guide. You can't get where you need to go without it.

My Prayer to God
Lord, thank You for dying for me, rising again, and coming to be in my heart. Thank You for making it clear to me my calling and my future. Please teach me how to be a better disciple and learn more of Your Word and understand more about You so I can bring more people to You.

(Age 14)

Prayer Power

Lord, thank You that "Your word is a lamp to my feet and a light to my path" (Psalm 119:105). I also know that it is food for my soul and I can't live without it. Help me to understand it whenever I read it. Show me the hidden treasures buried in it. Teach me things I need to see. Show me what You want me to know. Help me to read something in Your Word every day. Help me to memorize certain verses. Change me as I read it. I don't want to be just a hearer of Your Word; I want to be a doer also. Help me to do the things Your Word says to do. Show me when I am not doing what it says.

I pray that Your Word will cleanse my heart and correct any wrong attitude I have. I pray it will give me hope and the ability to rise above my limitations. I pray it will prepare me to move into the purpose You have for me on this earth. I pray it will increase my faith and remind me of who You are and how much You love me.

Thank You, Lord, that when I look in Your Word I can see You more clearly. Help me to hear Your voice speaking to my heart every time I read or hear it. I don't want to ever miss the way You are leading me. In Jesus' name I pray.

WORD POWER

The word of God is living and powerful, and sharper than any two-edged sword...and is a discerner of the thoughts and intents of the heart.
HEBREWS 4:12

He who heeds the word wisely will find good, and whoever trusts in the LORD, happy is he.
PROVERBS 16:20

Blessed is the man who walks not in the counsel of the ungodly, nor stands in the path of sinners, nor sits in the seat of the scornful; but his delight is in the law of the LORD, and in His law he meditates day and night. He shall be like a tree planted by the rivers of water, that brings forth its fruit in its season, whose leaf also shall not wither; and whatever he does shall prosper.

PSALM 1:1-3

1 The most difficult thing for me about reading God's Word every day is:

2 The most difficult thing to me about understanding God's Word is:

3 The three Scriptures I most want to memorize so that I can always have God's Word in my heart are:

'LORD, HELP ME'

Be Free from Peer Pressure

I ONCE HEARD A RADIO INTERVIEW WITH some gang members in Los Angeles, where I used to live. At the time, crime was extremely high in that city because of a terrifying wave of random drive-by shootings and murders committed by gangs. The talk show host was interviewing these boys, some barely teenagers and some in their early twenties. They said that the main reason they joined their gang was to have a sense of belonging. In bone-chilling statements, a number of the boys admitted they would do whatever it took to be accepted and respected by the group. Even commit murder.

Some of the boys revealed that the main test of whether they could be accepted into the gang was to go out and kill someone. Anyone. The murder was entirely random. There was no other reason for the murder other than to complete the initiation requirement and prove that they would do anything for the group. Some of the boys being interviewed confessed that they hated doing that and wished there had been another way to become a member. But they were so desperate to belong to a family of people where they felt accepted that they went ahead with it. This was a frightening revelation to all of us who lived there because it meant no place was safe.

Around that same time, a friend of ours was out in front of his own home in broad daylight when he was approached by two young boys. They were walking down the street, which was in a very nice and quiet residential neighborhood, when one of the boys pulled out a gun and shot our friend point-blank. There was no robbery or attempt to commit any other crime, and the boys fled away on foot. Our friend lived through it, but the damage to his body greatly affected his ability to do the work he was an expert in doing, and it took him years to recover.

It was obvious that these young boys in the interview had no sense of purpose for their lives outside of belonging to a gang. Most of them were raised without fathers, and in some cases the mother was absent too. I'm sure that if each of them would have had a strong sense of family, and love and acceptance from other people, they would never have chosen this destructive lifestyle.

This story illustrates how desperately people need other people. And how much they need the Lord. Everybody needs to feel accepted. We all desperately need a sense of family, of relationship, of belonging. If you don't realize that about yourself, it's probably because you have always had that. God created us to be in families. We have a natural hunger to be a part of something that gives us a sense of acceptance, affirmation, and being needed and appreciated. But teenagers feel that more strongly than people of any other age. When young people are deprived of good, healthy, godly, supportive relationships, they will seek ones that aren't. That's how they get in with the wrong crowd. That's how gangs are formed.

The Rules of Acceptance

As a teenager, the feeling of acceptance by your peers is one of the most important things in your life. Not recognizing that need for acceptance can get you into trouble if you don't realize how strong social pressure can be at your age. I don't think it is ever as strong at any other time of life.

The unwritten social rules for teenagers are often very strict, and peers can be cruel and intolerant when someone violates those rules. For example, in some places a violation of this social structure happens if a person isn't wearing the right thing from the right place and doesn't look a certain way. Not looking the "accepted way" can keep that person from being accepted in the stratosphere of the elite. Or if a person doesn't act a certain way, accomplish certain things, or have certain abilities, they may not be accepted by a particular group. Adults experience some of that too, but they have the freedom to find their niche in life and be where they are most comfortable. Teenagers don't usually have that freedom. They have to make the best of where they are and who they are with. And that can be very difficult.

Being accepted is a big issue, and not feeling accepted can be the root of many problems in a young person's life. Any sense of rejection can be devastating, and the memory of it can torture someone for years to come. Whether or not you are accepted by other people influences how you feel about yourself and your life. Not being accepted by the people you want to be accepted by can make you feel like you have to try and be accepted by other people who may not be at all reflective of who you really are. That's what happened to those gang members who were interviewed. The

The Main Things I Pray About Are:

- That I can know God better
- That God will forgive me
- For purity in my relationships
- For the renewing of my mind
- For the salvation of my family and friends

(Ages 16-19)

things the gang leaders required of them was not something they wanted to do, but their desire to be accepted was stronger than their sense of right and wrong.

That's what peer pressure is: Conforming to what other people your own age want in order to gain their acceptance. It's fearing the opinions of others. And it can be extremely unhealthy for your life when it causes you to do things you wouldn't normally do in order to win the approval of a certain group of people. Of course, this gang illustration is an extreme example of that, but it shows how strong peer pressure is.

If you sense intense peer pressure from the people you are around, I understand the difficulty in that. But there is a way to become strong enough to be free of it. Not that it won't be there, but it won't matter so much to you.

Rejection by certain people can be very painful. And because your world is so small, it may seem as though there is no escaping from it. When you are in tenth grade, the three years looming ahead of you before you can graduate and leave that situation can seem like an eternity. But God doesn't want you suffering in an uncomfortable social situation because the pressure of peers is making you miserable. He doesn't want you tolerating the problem or barely making it through. He wants you to be able to rise above it. And you *can* when you realize how much you are accepted and loved by God and when you understand the power of your prayers to change situations.

Problems happen when you try to live up to other people's standard for your life instead of God's. The way to avoid that is to make *His* standard a priority in your life and spend time with other people who do the same.

Setting Your Priorities

We can live happy and successful lives if we have our priorities completely clear in our mind. If our priorities aren't straight, we will be led around by the expectations of our peers. Correct priorities are not something we can figure out on our own. We have to know what *God* says they should be. We need to have a clear knowledge of God's Word and the leading of His Holy Spirit.

Our two most important priorities come directly from the Word of God. They are:

Priority **1**: Love God

Priority **2**: Love others

> **I Prayed and God Answered**
> My family and I prayed four years ago for a daughter/sister and God gave me a little sister.
> (Age 14)

Jesus told us about these two top priorities saying, "'You shall love the LORD your God with all your heart, with all your soul, and with all your mind.' This is the first and great commandment. And the second is like it: 'You shall love your neighbor as yourself'" (Matthew **22:37-39**). It can't get much clearer than that. If you maintain these two top priorities—love God and love others—they will guide you in setting all the other priorities in your life.

Your relationship with the Lord must always have top priority over everything else. When the Lord said, "You shall have no other gods before Me" (Exodus **20:3**), He meant it. God wants your undivided attention. When you seek Him first every day and ask Him to help you put your life in order, He will do that. I know from experience, and I'm sure you do too, that when we don't seek God first, our life gets out of control. When that happens to you, then life starts ruling *you* instead of you ruling *it*. People start influencing you more than God does.

God is a God of order. We can tell that by looking at the universe. None of it is random or accidental. He doesn't want our lives to be either of those things. His will is that we "let all things be done decently and in order" (1 Corinthians 14:40). And when we pray to Him about it, He will help us do just that. He will show us how to align ourselves under proper authority so that we can come under the covering of His protection. This is crucial to resisting peer pressure.

Knowing Whom It Is You Serve

Submission is a condition of the heart. It is something you *decide* to do, not something someone forces you to do. Having a submitted heart means you are willing to come into proper alignment in accordance with God's will.

Our first priority in submission must always be to "submit to God" (James 4:7). This means you do not have to submit to the wishes of anyone who tries to pressure you to do something that is against God's laws. You can have a submitted heart and still be able to draw the line when what is being asked of you violates your conscience and the laws of God.

Jesus Himself was submitted to God. It would seem that if anyone would not have to be in perfect submission to God, it would be Jesus. But in order to accomplish God's purpose for His life, He was submitted to the will of the Father, even to the point of suffering and death. God wants "this mind [to] be in you which was also in Christ Jesus" (Philippians 2:5-8). That doesn't mean you have to die, because Jesus already did that. It means you have to make God's will your first priority. What *He* wants is more important than what anyone else may be pressuring you to do.

Submitting to Others

Beyond submission to God, the Bible says you should submit to authority figures designated by God in your family, your church, your work, and your government. You need to submit first of all to your parents. Life is going to be miserable for you if you don't. You also need to submit to your teachers, your principal, your pastor, and the police. Submission means doing what that person wants. But you should never submit to anyone when you know they are asking you to do something that violates the laws of God and your conscience. And that includes even these important people in your life.

If a person who is a designated authority over you asks you to do something that is wrong, or if that person says or does something to you that is inappropriate and violates what is right in the sight of God, you must decline to be a part of it and declare it to be wrong. God never wants you to be the object of another person's abuse or misdirection. If you find yourself going along with someone who is violating the Word of God or the laws of your world, not to mention your own conscience, that's not submission. That's just dumb. Don't go there.

When you go along with what your peers are doing even though you know it isn't right, then you are submitting yourself to them and not to God. I've heard young men and women both admit that they had sex as a teenager, even though they didn't want to, just because everyone else was doing it and they wanted to be accepted. Submit to God and the authorities He has put in your life and you won't submit to peer pressure.

Don't Be the Peer Putting on the Pressure

Beyond submission to God and submission to other designated authorities in your life, you must be in right relationship to other people, "submitting to one another in the fear of God"

(Ephesians 5:21). Submission to others takes a heart that loves other people as yourself. It means respecting them as human beings. It means treating them politely. It means not snubbing them or treating them rudely because they don't look the same as you. It means being nice to anyone you see being mistreated, and standing up for them against those who mistreat them.

This is a serious issue. Terrible and hurtful things have happened to people as a result of having been treated with rejection by other people. The ultimate result is death and destruction. The worst examples are the numerous cases of boys who felt rejected and ended up killing their peers and themselves in school massacres. Perhaps you can do something to help prevent these kinds of things from happening in *your* world by praying for people you see who are being rejected. Because you are in that world, you can see what adults are not seeing. Ask God to show you if someone around you is slipping through the cracks because they feel rejected by their peers. When God reveals someone, pray for that person that he or she will find acceptance. Pray they will find the Lord and come to an understanding about His purpose for their lives. Ask God if He wants you to be an instrument of His love to see that accomplished.

I Prayed and God Answered

I really missed my old friends at my new school. So I asked God to make me feel more comfortable. Now I enjoy my school a lot more now.
(Age 13)

God is a God of love, and He asks us to behave lovingly toward others. God didn't say that you have to be best friends with everyone. He said you have to love them. He will give you a heart to do that. When you have a heart that loves and cares about people enough to respect and accept them as a child of God like you are, it is a very popular quality that draws other people to you.

Sometimes just a smile and an acknowledgment of someone's presence can change their entire day. Maybe even the course of their life. You have the power to do that because you are a child of God and the Holy Spirit lives in you. God will use you as an instrument of peace if you ask Him to.

When you love God first and others second, all the other priorities in your life will fall into place. And when you have your priorities in order, peers can't pressure you to do anything that doesn't please God.

My Prayer to God

Lord, I pray that You will give me strength, courage, and energy to keep doing well in school. Instill in me Your mighty power so that I can be an impact to others.

(Age 15)

Prayer Power

Lord, help me to always put You first in my life. Teach me how to love You with all my heart, mind, and soul. Show me when I am not doing that. I submit my life to You. Help me to always submit to the authorities You have put in my life. Help me to resist the pressure of peers to be a part of anything that is not pleasing in Your sight. Help me to judge myself by *Your* standards and not theirs.

Reveal to me anyone in my world who is suffering from feelings of rejection and show me how to pray for them. Make me aware and show me how I can be an instrument of Your love and peace to them.

I know that if my life is not in proper order, I will not receive all that You have for me. I also know that if I seek You first, all that I need will be given to me (Matthew 6:33). I seek You first this day and ask that You would enable me to put my life in perfect order. In Jesus' name I pray.

WORD POWER

Seek first the kingdom of God and His righteousness, and all these things shall be added to you.

MATTHEW **6:33**

He who finds his life will lose it, and he who loses his life for My sake will find it.

MATTHEW **10:39**

Obey those who rule over you, and be submissive, for they watch out for your souls, as those who must give account. Let them do so with joy and not with grief, for that would be unprofitable for you.

HEBREWS **13:17**

1

The way I most sense peer pressure in my life is:

2

The ways I can put God first in my life are:

3

Write out a prayer asking God to show you who the authority figures are in your life and what you can do to be in
submission to them. Ask Him to show you anyone who
feels rejected and needs your prayers.

chapter 9

'LORD, HELP ME'
Have Good Relationships

THERE IS NOTHING MORE IMPORTANT IN the life of a teenager than having good, godly friends. The Bible talks so much about the importance of having the right kind of friends that we can't treat this part of our lives lightly. It says that "the righteous should choose his friends carefully, for the way of the wicked leads them astray" (Proverbs 12:26). If it's true that we become like the friends we spend time with, then we must select our friends carefully. We should look carefully at our friends and ask ourselves, "Is that the kind of person I want to be like?" If not, we should ask God to help us get free of that relationship and bring someone better into our life.

The main quality to look for in a close friend is not how attractive, talented, wealthy, smart, influential, clever, or popular they

I Think of God As:

- My Savior
- My Provider
- My Creator
- My Friend
- My Lord
  (Ages 16-19)

are. It's how much they love and fear God. The person who will do what it takes to live in the perfect will of God is the kind of friend who will impart something of the goodness of the Lord to you every time you are with them.

God doesn't want us to be unequally yoked with unbelievers. That doesn't mean we should never have anything to do with people who don't know Him. Far from it. We are God's tool to reach others for His kingdom. But our closest relationships, the ones that influence us the most, need to be with people who love and fear God. If you don't have close friends who are believers, ask God to send you some. He will do that. Use the following signs of desirable and undesirable friends to help you see the truth about your relationships.

Seven Signs of a Desirable Friend

1. *A desirable friend tells you the truth in love.* "Faithful are the wounds of a friend, but the kisses of an enemy are deceitful" (Proverbs 27:6).

2. *A desirable friend gives you sound advice.* "Ointment and perfume delight the heart, and the sweetness of a man's friend gives delight by hearty counsel" (Proverbs 27:9).

3. *A desirable friend helps you become a better person.* "As iron sharpens iron, so a man sharpens the countenance of his friend" (Proverbs 27:17).

4. *A desirable friend helps you become a wiser person.* "He who walks with wise men will be wise, but the companion of fools will be destroyed" (Proverbs 13:20).

5. *A desirable friend remains close to you, even in the tough times.* "A man who has friends must himself be friendly, but there is a friend who sticks closer than a brother" (Proverbs 18:24).

6. *A desirable friend loves you and stands by you, even when you do stupid things.* "A friend loves at all times, and a brother is born for adversity" (Proverbs 17:17).

7. *A desirable friend helps you when you are having trouble in your life so you won't have to go through it alone.* "Two are better than one, because they have a good reward for their labor. For if they fall, one will lift up his companion. But woe to him who is alone when he falls, for he has no one to help him up" (Ecclesiastes 4:9-10).

The Main Things I Pray About Are:
- My parents and my family
- For a future spouse
- That I can make good friends
- That I will live in sexual purity
- That God will help me tell others about Him

(Ages 13-15)

If you have friends with the qualities listed above, protect those friendships with prayer. If you have friends who have any of the undesirable qualities listed below, you need to pray about them as well. Ask God if they are the people He wants you to spend time with or not. If not, ask Him to take those relationships out of your life and bring new ones to you that are better.

Seven Signs of an Undesirable Friend

1. *An undesirable friend is ungodly and doesn't care if he hurts other people.* "I have written to you not to keep company with anyone named a brother, who is sexually immoral, or covetous, or an idolater, or a reviler, or a drunkard, or an extortioner—not even to eat with such a person" (1 Corinthians 5:11).

2. *An undesirable friend is changeable and unstable, and you never know how that person is going to act from one day to the next.* "Do not associate with those given to change; for their calamity

will rise suddenly, and who knows the ruin those two can bring?" (Proverbs 24:21-22).

3. *An undesirable friend is often angry about something.* "Make no friendship with an angry man, and with a furious man do not go, lest you learn his ways and set a snare for your soul" (Proverbs 22:24-25).

4. *An undesirable friend gives you bad and ungodly advice.* "Blessed is the man who walks not in the counsel of the ungodly, nor stands in the path of sinners, nor sits in the seat of the scornful" (Psalm 1:1).

5. *An undesirable friend is an unbeliever who doesn't obey the law.* "Do not be unequally yoked together with unbelievers. For what fellowship has righteousness with lawlessness? And what communion has light with darkness? And what accord has Christ with Belial? Or what part has a believer with an unbeliever?" (2 Corinthians 6:14-15).

6. *An undesirable friend does foolish things; a fool does things without thinking through what the consequences will be.* "He who walks with wise men will be wise, but the companion of fools will be destroyed" (Proverbs 13:20).

7. *An undesirable friend is not reverent toward God and His laws.* "I am a companion of all who fear You, and of those who keep Your precepts" (Psalm 119:63).

The Importance of Having a Spiritual Family

God is our Father. We are His kids. That means we who are believers in Jesus are all brothers and sisters. There are too many of us to all live in the same house, so God puts us in separate houses. We call them churches. Our relationships within these church families are crucial to our well-being. How we relate to the other people there will greatly affect the quality of our life in the Lord. We can never reach our full destiny apart from the godly people He puts in our lives. I don't mean these people will necessarily help us do what we do, but our relationships with them will contribute to our success.

We all have blind spots. We all need people who will help us see the truth about ourselves and our lives. We need people to tell us if we are getting off track. And we need to have the kind of relationships that don't break down when truth is spoken in love.

This doesn't mean you will never have a problem in any of your church relationships, or that if you do it's a sign you are in the wrong place. All relationships have things that need to be worked out. Getting beyond those problems makes relationships rich. But we have to learn to protect our relationships with our spiritual family in prayer.

Going to a good church is extremely important. It gives you the best environment where healthy relationships can form. If you aren't going to a church now, ask God to show you where you should go. If you are extremely unhappy at the church where you attend now, ask your parents to help you find another church. If they object to you changing churches because they want you to attend with them, then do what they are asking you to do. Keeping the family together is important. If you still feel it is not the right place for you, ask God to change their hearts about it, or at least open their hearts to listen to you.

I tell parents that one of the most

> **I Prayed and God Answered**
>
> One night I prayed that my friend would realize his life was going off the deep end. He called me that night and said "My life is going off the deep end" and gave his life to Christ. I knew my prayers were powerful then.
>
> (Age 18)

> **I Prayed and God Answered**
>
> My mom couldn't have more children but I prayed to have a little brother and a few months later she was pregnant with a boy.
>
> (Age 13)

My Prayer to God
Lord, help me to tell people about You.
(Age 13)

important things for a teenager is that they attend a good Bible-teaching church that they like, with a youth group that they enjoy. If your church doesn't have one and your friend's church does, ask your parents if they would allow you to attend your friend's youth group. Invite them to go there too so they can check it out and feel comfortable with it. But respect their final decision, because God gives them wisdom as parents that you always need to honor. The bottom line is staying in church must be a priority. What you have to face as a teenager is too difficult without the support of a good spiritual family in the Lord.

Keep in mind that your enemy doesn't want you to be in a spiritual family or have godly relationships. That's because he knows how beneficial they are for you. He knows that without a spiritual family you won't grow properly. He knows if you are not joined and committed to a good church, you will end up living in rebellion in some way whether you mean to or not. He knows you will never be all God created you to be if you are not connected to other people who love the Lord in a deep and meaningful way.

Praying for Your Relationships

Don't leave your relationships to chance. Pray for each one. It's easier to protect them in prayer first than it is to fix them later. Ask God to help you be a good friend to others and to give you a pure and loving heart in all your relationships. Pray for godly people to come into your life with whom you can connect. Don't force relationships to happen; *pray* for them to happen.

Throughout your whole life, relationships will be crucial to your happiness. Good relationships will make your life richer and more balanced and give you a more positive outlook. Godly people will help you walk in the right direction. The good in them will rub off on you. The quality of your relationships will determine the quality of your life. And this is something worth praying about.

Prayer Power

Lord, I lift every one of my relationships up to You and ask You to bless each one. Help me to choose my friends wisely so that I won't be led astray. Give me discernment and strength to separate myself from anyone who is not a good influence.

I pray for my relationship with each of my family members. Specifically, I pray for my relationship with (name the family member with whom you are most concerned). I pray You would restore the relationship I have with that person so it will be good and strong. May Your forgiveness and love flow between us.

I pray for godly friends, role models, and mentors to come into my life. Send people who will be trustworthy, kind, and loving. Most of all I pray that they will be people who have strong faith in You and who will inspire me to have stronger faith too. Help me to always be in the right church so that I can be connected to a good strong church family. In Jesus' name I pray.

Word Power

Let all bitterness, wrath, anger, clamor, and evil speaking be put away from you, with all malice. And be kind to one another, tenderhearted, forgiving one another, just as God in Christ forgave you.

EPHESIANS 4:31-32

And this commandment we have from Him: that he who loves God must love his brother also.

1 JOHN 4:21

God sets the lonely in families.

PSALM 68:6 NIV

1 List all of the friends and family members whom you want to pray for regularly.

2 Think of your closest friends. Are you a desirable friend to those people? Check the lists of desirable and undesirable friends on pages 102-104. Do you have any of the undesirable traits? If so, list them in a prayer asking God to help you get rid of those traits. If not, ask Him to help you be the best friend you can be.

3 Are you friends with anyone you feel is not a good influence in your life? Someone who falls in the Undesirable Friend category? If so, write out a prayer asking God to either change that person or take them out of your life. If you can't think of anyone like that, write out a prayer asking God to reveal any friendship that is having a negative effect on you.

chapter 10

'LORD, HELP ME'

Praise You at All Times

WHEN I LIVED IN CALIFORNIA, I WORKED as a singer and dancer on television. I would have to sing a song over and over all day long while I was rehearsing it with the choreography. I used to go home at night and could hardly sleep because the music and lyrics of the songs we had been working on would still be playing over and over in my mind. I could not get them out of my head.

That is what happens to us when we hear and sing praise and worship songs over and over. They continue to play in our mind, soul, and spirit, even when we are not actually worshiping God. Even when we are sleeping.

I learned that principle years ago when I first became a believer. Back when I suffered with fear and depression, many times I would wake up with a terrible feeling of fear, anxiety, and dread, and I would sing or speak praise to God until those feelings went away. It amazed me that praise always worked.

I had gone to several doctors about the fear, depression, and anxiety I felt, but the medicine they gave me that was supposed to help only seemed to cover up the problem, not get rid of it. The problem was still there when the medicine wore off. I'm not saying that people shouldn't take medicine if they are depressed. I'm saying it didn't solve the problem for me. I had suffered from depression from the time I was a young child and was locked in a closet by my mother. The hopelessness, futility, and sadness I felt about myself and my life made it hard to get through each day. I needed an infusion of the joy of the Lord, and that's what praising God did for me.

When I praised and worshiped God, it was like being hooked up to a spiritual IV. As long as I had my heart and eyes lifted to Him in worship and praise, the joy of the Lord poured into my mind, soul, and spirit and crowded out the darkness and depression. It worked every time.

I Feel Most Like Praying When:
- I have a concern
- I don't know what to do
- I am tired spiritually
- I am thankful
- I sense the Holy Spirit is with me

(Ages 16-19)

I started buying praise and worship songs to play in the car as I drove, in my bedroom before I went to bed, in the bathroom when I was getting ready to go some place, in the kitchen as I was cooking something to eat, throughout the house where I was living, and if possible, in the place where I was working. Sometimes I would sing along with them, but other times I would just let the music play through my mind and spirit. It amazed me that confusion, oppression, fear, or anxiety couldn't exist in the same room where praise music was being played or sung. Eventually, I got completely free from all of those negative emotions, but I still played worship music whenever I wanted to have peace and a greater sense of God's presence.

I was very surprised when I found out about the power of praising God. I learned that anytime I start feeling bad or sad or mad, if I praise God for who He is and all He has done, those feelings will go away. Nothing we do is more powerful or more life changing. It is one of the ways God transforms us and our circumstances. Every time we praise and worship God, His presence comes to be with us and changes our attitude. It allows the Holy Spirit to soften and mold our heart into whatever way He wants it to be.

I Believe in Prayer Because:

- My prayers have been answered before
- It gets me what I need emotionally and spiritually
- God always listens to my prayers
- It is the only way I can talk to God
- God did a miracle in my life when I prayed before (Ages 13-15)

Because praise and worship is not something we naturally want to do, we have to will ourselves to do it. And because it's not the first thing we think of, we have to decide to do it no matter what is going in our lives. If we are having a bad day, instead of allowing ourselves to feel miserable, we have to say, "I will praise the Lord at all times." Of course, the more we get to know God, the easier praise becomes. And the more we understand what is accomplished in our lives when we praise Him, the more we won't be able to keep from praising Him. If you ever find that you don't feel like praising God, read the following 20 reasons to worship God from Psalm 103.

Twenty Reasons to Praise God Now

1. He forgives my sins.
2. He heals my sicknesses.

3. He saves me from destruction.
4. He gives me love and kindness.
5. He gives me good food to eat.
6. He sees that justice is done.
7. He shows me how to live.
8. He gives me mercy.
9. He is gracious to me.
10. He is slow to anger.
11. He will not strive with me.
12. He will not be angry with me.
13. He does not punish me like I deserve.
14. He shows special mercy when I worship Him.
15. He takes away all of my sins.
16. He has pity on me.
17. He remembers what I'm made of.
18. His mercy toward me lasts forever.
19. He blesses me when I obey Him.
20. He is the ruler of everything.

I Prayed and God Answered

I cracked four discs in my back in a gymnastics accident and was told I would never be able to do gymnastics or dance again. I prayed for healing. Two months later there was no sign of any problem.

(Age 15)

We can claim to know and love God, but if we are not worshiping and praising Him every day, we are in the dark about who He really is. "Although they knew God, they did not glorify Him as God, nor were thankful, but became futile in their thoughts, and their foolish hearts were darkened" (Romans 1:21). We shut off so much in our lives when we don't give praise to God like we should. We don't want to be wandering around in the dark, entertaining futility in our minds, all because we are not worshiping God.

Praise Can Lift You Higher

Just like a bird knows how to find the right air current so it can be lifted off the ground and fly, there is a way for you to be lifted up so you can soar too. That is through praise and worship. And the most powerful time for that is together with other believers. When you are in a worship service at church, in a youth group, in a meeting, or in a gathering with other Christians, powerful things happen in your life and in your soul that might not happen at any other time. The Bible says, "In the presence of the congregation I will sing your praises" (Hebrews 2:12 NIV). Don't neglect to have times of praise alongside other believers, because as you lift God up in praise, the Holy Spirit will also lift your spirit and you will soar above everything else in your life.

Remember to "rejoice always, pray without ceasing, in everything give thanks; for this is the will of God in Christ Jesus for you" (1 Thessalonians 5:16-18). Make praise your *first* reaction to the difficult things that happen to you and not an afterthought. God is always worthy of praise no matter what is happening in your life.

I Prayed and God Answered

I was living in another country, but I prayed that God would get me into the United States. When God sent a special person to help me do that, then I knew God was real and listening to me.

(Age 16)

Prayer Power

Lord, there is nothing that makes me happier than worshiping You. I invite Your presence right now as I come before You with praise for how wonderful You are. I thank You for all that You have done for me. You are great and worthy to be praised. Lord, I Thank You that "You have put gladness in my heart" (Psalm 4:7).

Thank You that You are my Healer, my Deliverer, my Provider, my Redeemer, my Father, and my Comforter. Thank You for revealing Yourself to me through Your Word; through Your Son, Jesus; and through Your Holy Spirit. Thank You for Your love, peace, joy, faithfulness, grace, mercy, kindness, truth, and healing. Thank You that I can depend on You because You and Your Word are unfailing. Thank You that You are the same yesterday, today, and tomorrow.

I praise Your name this day, Lord, for You are good and Your mercy endures forever (Psalm 136:1). "Because Your lovingkindness is better than life, my lips shall praise You. Thus I will bless You while I live; I will lift up my hands in Your name" (Psalm 63:3-4). Teach me to worship You with my whole heart the way You want me to. Help me to make praise and worship of You be my first response to everything that happens to me. In Jesus' name I pray.

My Prayer to God

Lord, there is nothing more I want than to fulfill Your destiny for my life. Help me, keep me strong, cover me with Your grace, steer me in Your path. In all I do, help me to worship You.

(Age 17)

WORD POWER

But the hour is coming, and now is, when the true worshipers will worship the Father in spirit and truth; for the Father is seeking such to worship Him. God is Spirit, and those who worship Him must worship in spirit and truth.

JOHN 4:23-24

Offer to God thanksgiving, and pay your vows to the Most High. Call upon Me in the day of trouble; I will deliver you, and you shall glorify Me.

PSALM 50:14-15

Let all those rejoice who put their trust in You; let them ever shout for joy, because You defend them; let those also who love Your name be joyful in You. For You, O LORD, will bless the righteous; with favor You will surround him as with a shield.

PSALM 5:11-12

1 What are you most thankful to God for today? Write it out as a prayer of praise to God below. (For example, "Lord, I am most thankful to You for . . .")

2 Remember the list of God's names in chapter **1** on pages 22-23? Write out a prayer of praise to God choosing the names of the Lord that mean the most to you today.

3 Do you find it hard to praise God when troubling things are happening to you? Think of the last time something hurtful or troubling happened to you and how you reacted to it. Now describe below how you could react with praise the next time something hurtful or upsetting happens. What could you praise God for?

chapter 11

'LORD, HELP ME'

Find Your Purpose for My Life

WHEN I WAS A TEENAGER, I DIDN'T KNOW God had a purpose for my life. I didn't know He had great things for me to do for His kingdom. If I had known all that, I would never have wasted my time doing destructive things and ending up in serious trouble. I don't want you to waste any part of your life doing that. I want you to know who you are in the Lord. I want you to be certain that God has a plan and a high purpose for your life so that you can move into it right away.

I've had so many people in their twenties and thirties tell me how they wasted years trying to figure out what they were supposed to be doing, and now they feel they've missed out on the purpose God had for their lives. I tell them, "No matter how far off the path you've gotten from the plans and purposes God has for you, when you surrender your life to the Lord, He carves a path from where you are to where you are *supposed* to be, and He puts you on it. It may take you longer to get where you are supposed to go than it would have if you had never gotten off the path from the beginning, but if you keep walking closely with God, He *will* get you where you are supposed to be. And you will see His purpose for your life be fulfilled."

The Bible tells us that "The gifts and the calling of God are irrevocable" (Romans **11:29**). That means He won't take back the gifts and abilities He gives you. They won't be recalled, repealed, or annulled. You will always have your gifts. He will always use them for His kingdom when you submit them to Him.

Everyone Has a Purpose

Every one of us has a purpose in the Lord, but not everyone realizes that. When we don't have a good understanding of who God made us to be, we strive to be like someone we're not. We compare ourselves to others and feel as though we always fall short. When we don't become who we think we're supposed to be, it makes us critical of ourselves and our lives. It causes us to be insecure, oversensitive, judgmental, frustrated, and unfulfilled. We become self-absorbed, constantly having to think about ourselves and what we should be. It forces us to try too hard to make life happen the way we think it is *supposed* to. In the extreme, it makes us tell lies about ourselves and become dishonest about who we really are.

The Hardest Thing About Prayer Is:

- Not knowing if God really hears me
- Not knowing if my prayers will be answered
- Letting my guard down to let the Spirit in
- Praying for others besides myself
- Knowing I won't always get what I want

(Ages 16-19)

When you're around people who don't have any idea about who they are and what they are called to do, you sense their unrest, unfulfillment, anxiety, and lack of peace. It makes you uncomfortable around them. God doesn't want that for you. He wants you to have a clear vision for your life. He wants to reveal to you what your gifts and talents are and show you how to best develop them and use them for His glory.

Ask God to Bless the Work You Do

Everybody has some kind of work to do. It doesn't matter if you are a full-time student, a babysitter, a house sitter, a volunteer at a rescue mission, or the head of your own business. Your work is important. It doesn't matter if you are getting paid big bucks or you are working for next to nothing or for free. Your work is valuable. It doesn't matter if your work is recognized by the whole world, by just a few people, or only by God. Your work makes a difference.

Whatever work you are doing, even if it is only a temporary job, you want to do it well, and you want it to be successful. If you are a student, studying is your job. You are not getting paid for it in money, but you are getting paid for it with good grades, self-respect, good opportunities

I Feel Most Like Praying When:
- I am alone
- I am feeling discouraged
- Before I go to bed
- God tells me to
- I see others hurting
  (Ages 13-15)

in your future, and satisfaction that you have done well. When the work you do is good, it makes you feel good about yourself and your life. Even if it's something you think is not important, it is still preparing you in some way for what God has for you in the future.

The Bible tells us that "the laborer is worthy of his wages" (1 Timothy 5:18). This means you deserve to be paid or rewarded for your work. Sometimes the reward is in the result. You don't get paid for cleaning your bedroom, serving soup at the rescue mission, or teaching a child to tie his shoes, but your reward for seeing the result of your labor is priceless. "The labor of the righteous leads to life" (Proverbs 10:16). No matter what your work is, it's important to God, it's important to others, and it's important to you. Commit your work to the Lord and ask Him to bless it.

Security Is Knowing Who You Are and Where You Are Going

Predestination means your destination has already been determined. The Bible says we are predestined according to God's purposes and will (Ephesians 1:11). That means God knows where you are supposed to be going. And He knows how to get you there. But even though you have a destiny, you can't get to it without being connected to the Lord who gave it to you in the first place.

When you don't stay connected to God, then in a moment of weakness, such as passion or anger, you can sell out your destiny. We see people on the news all the time who do that. Any criminal who robs and murders and destroys has no clue about who God made him to be. If he clearly understood that God has a high purpose for his life, he wouldn't throw it away with such foolish actions and decisions.

When you understand God has a purpose for your life, you won't be insecure about your future. He will enable you to do what you need to do. *Because of God's greatness in you, He can accomplish great things*

The Main Things I Pray About Are:

- Getting into a good college
- Communicating better with my parents
- For God to reveal His will to me
- For my destiny, my future, and my purpose
- For protection for me and my family

(Ages 16-19)

120

through you. When you know you are the Lord's, and you trust where He is taking you, you feel very secure.

We Are All Called to Help Others

One of the things we are all called to do is give of ourselves to other people. Giving to God and to other people is such a vitally important part of our life on this earth that we can never achieve all we want to see happen in our lives if we're not doing that. When we give to God and to others, it creates a vacuum into which God pours more blessings. If we stop up that flow, we stop up our lives.

One of the greatest things you can give to someone is your prayers for them. You can pray for their protection, health, salvation, family, finances, or whatever else they might need. Praying for others is called intercessory prayer. This is one part of our calling that we all have in common because we are all called to intercede for others. Prayer is the greatest gift. I would rather have someone pray for me than anything else they could give me. Don't forget that part of your calling in life is to pray for others.

I Prayed and God Answered

I didn't have friends at the beginning of the year. I asked God to give me one good friend. Now I have a best friend, and she has helped me to turn my life around and get my life on the right track.

(Age 14)

Surrendering Your Dreams

You can never move into all God has for you and become all He created you to be without surrendering your dreams to Him. Jesus said, "Whoever desires to save his life will lose it, but whoever loses his life for My sake will find it" (Matthew 16:25). That means if you want to have a life that is secure in the Lord, you have to let go of your plans and say, "Not *my* will, but *Yours* be done, Lord."

This is hard to do, because letting go of your dreams is the last thing you want to do. But if you ask God to take away the dreams in your heart that are not from Him and bring to pass the ones that are, you can't go wrong. If you have a dream that is not of God, when you surrender it to Him, He will take away your desire for it and give you what *He* desires for you. This can be very painful, especially if it is a dream you've been clinging to for a long time. But you don't want to spend your life chasing after a dream that God will not bless. You will be constantly frustrated if you do, and the dream will never be realized.

My Prayer to God
Lord, please show me Your will and open doors in others' lives to understand Your will too.
(Age 14)

You always want to be living out the dreams *God* puts in your heart. Even if the dreams you have in your heart right now *are* from God, you will still have to surrender them. That's because He wants you clinging to *Him* and not to your dreams. He doesn't want you trying to *make* them happen. He wants you to trust Him so *He* can make them happen.

Finding Your Purpose

We all need to have a sense of why we are here. We all need to know we were created for a purpose. We will never find fulfillment and happiness until we are doing the thing for which we were created. But God won't move us into the big things He has called us to unless we have been proven faithful in the small things He has given us. So if what you are doing right now seems to be a small thing in your eyes, be happy! God is getting you ready for big things ahead.

God has a purpose for you right now. He has something for you to do today. If you are not sure what God wants you to do today, ask Him to show you and then do what He speaks to your heart. When you are faithful in a few small things, He will move you into bigger things.

Concerning the call of God upon your life, the Bible says that God "has saved us and called us with a holy calling, not according to our works, but according to His own purpose and grace which was given to us in Christ Jesus before time began" (2 Timothy 1:9). "Having then gifts differing according to the grace that is given to us, let us use them" (Romans 12:6). For "each one has his own gift from God, one in this manner and another in that" (1 Corinthians 7:7). So then, "as God has distributed to each one, as the Lord has called each one, so let him walk" (1 Corinthians 7:17). I pray that God will "give to you the spirit of wisdom and revelation in the knowledge of Him, the eyes of your understanding being enlightened; that you may know what is the hope of His calling" (Ephesians 1:17-18). "May He grant you according to your heart's desire, and fulfill all your purpose" (Psalm 20:4).

Remember that God has important things for you to do with your life, and He has placed gifts, talents, and abilities in you for that purpose. It doesn't matter if anyone else sees them at this point. God reveals them to others when He is ready to do so.

Prayer Power

Lord, thank You that You have a plan and a purpose for my life. I know that Your plan for me existed before I knew You, and You will bring it to pass. I know that I am called to serve and help others, so use me as Your instrument to make a positive difference. Show me what You want me to do to serve my family, friends, church, and the people You put in my life.

Help me to excel in my work so that the result of what I do will be pleasing to others. Open doors of opportunity to use my skills and close doors that I am not to go through. Give me wisdom and direction about that. Bless the work I am doing now and whatever You call me to in the future. Give me the ability to do it successfully.

I know that whatever You have called me to do, You will enable me to do it. I pray that nothing will draw me away from fulfilling the plan You have for me. I surrender my dreams to You. May I never stray from what You have called me to be and do. Give me a vision for my life and a strong sense of purpose. In Jesus' name I pray.

WORD
POWER

Walk worthy of the calling with which you were called, with all lowliness and gentleness, with longsuffering, bearing with one another in love, endeavoring to keep the unity of the Spirit in the bond of peace.

EPHESIANS 4:1-3

Be even more diligent to make your call and election sure, for if you do these things you will never stumble.

2 PETER 1:10

Let the beauty of the LORD our God be upon us, and establish the work of our hands for us; yes, establish the work of our hands.

PSALM 90:17

1 What are your gifts, talents, and abilities? Write down anything you like to do, want to do, are good at, or would like to learn to be good at.

2 What would you most like to do in your life? This doesn't mean you have to do it or that you won't change your mind later on, but usually the things that you enjoy doing will somehow be used to prepare you for what God is calling you to do.

3 Write out a prayer to God asking Him to reveal to you His calling upon your life. Ask Him to help you understand and develop the gifts and talents and abilities He has put in you.

chapter 12

'LORD, HELP ME'

Make Wise Choices

ONE TIME I SPENT A WEEK IN FLORIDA on vacation, and I stayed in a high-rise beachfront condominium. As I was standing out on the seventh-story balcony overlooking the ocean, I had an interesting view of the water below. From where I was, I could clearly see where the shallow places were, and where the ocean floor suddenly fell off and the water was very deep. I watched people swim out a ways and suddenly find themselves in a shallow place and be forced to stand up. The water at those shallow places was barely knee level. It was fascinating to watch the swimmers walk around on the sandy plateau and then suddenly fall over the edge into deep water.

I realized that if I could have been connected to each of those swimmers by a waterproof cell phone, I could have told them when they were near the edge so they wouldn't fall off. But they had no contact with me, so I couldn't tell them what I saw from my perspective.

That's the way it is with God. He sees all that's happening to us because He is above it all. If we were to connect with Him on a regular basis and say, "Lord, guide me so I won't fall," He could lead us away from the edge. But so often we don't make that call. We don't seek out His guidance. We don't ask Him for wisdom. We don't consider His perspective. And too often we fall in over our heads because of it.

A man named Lot, Abraham's nephew in the Bible, ended up being captured by the enemy because he chose to be in a place that he thought was a good place to live (Genesis 13:10-11). But it was among wicked people who would eventually be a big part of his downfall (Genesis 13:13). He chose what *he thought* was best, rather than asking what *God knew* was best. How many times do people walk out from under God's umbrella of protection and away from His best, all because they have chosen what they *think* is best for their lives? They don't ask for *God's* wisdom and direction. We all do that at one time or another. Unfortunately, we sometimes have to learn a few hard lessons first.

Have you ever observed someone with no wisdom clearly doing the wrong thing or making a foolish decision? The consequences are crystal clear to you, but they don't see it at all. It's always easier to see a lack of wisdom in someone else than it is to see it in ourselves. That's why we must pray for wisdom often.

Wisdom means having clear understanding and insight. It means knowing how to apply the truth in every situation. It's discerning what is right and wrong. It's having good

I Feel Most Like Praying When:
- I can
- I'm thinking of God
- I'm going through hard times
- I'm mad or angry
- I'm feeling down

(Ages 13-15)

judgment. It's being able to sense when you are getting too close to the edge. It's making the right choice or decision. And often only God knows what that is. "When He, the Spirit of truth, has come, He will guide you into all truth; for He will not speak on His own authority, but whatever He hears He will speak; and He will tell you things to come" (John 16:13).

I Think of God As:
- Good
- Holy
- Merciful
- Perfect
- Reliable
(Ages 16-19)

We have no idea how many times simple wisdom has saved our lives or kept us out of harm's way. Or how many times it will do so again in the future. That's why we need to ask God for wisdom to walk through every day.

Ten Ways to Walk in Wisdom

1. *Read the Bible.* "My son, if you receive my words, and treasure my commands within you, so that you incline your ear to wisdom, and apply your heart to understanding...then you will understand the fear of the LORD, and find the knowledge of God" (Proverbs 2:1-2,5).

2. *Pray for God to give you wisdom.* "If any of you lacks wisdom, let him ask of God, who gives to all liberally and without reproach, and it will be given to him" (James 1:5).

3. *Bring God into everything you do.* "In all your ways acknowledge Him, and He shall direct your paths" (Proverbs 3:6).

4. *Have reverence in your heart for God.* "The fear of the LORD is the beginning of wisdom" (Proverbs 9:10).

5. *Pay attention to what wise people say and do.* "Incline your ear and hear the words of the wise, and apply your heart to my knowledge" (Proverbs 22:17).

6. *Value wisdom more than anything else.* "Get wisdom! Get understanding! Do not forget, nor turn away from the words

129

of my mouth. Do not forsake her, and she will preserve you; love her, and she will keep you" (Proverbs 4:5-6).

7. *Live God's way.* "He stores up sound wisdom for the upright; He is a shield to those who walk uprightly" (Proverbs 2:7).

8. *Be humble.* "When pride comes, then comes shame; but with the humble is wisdom" (Proverbs 11:2).

9. *Love others and be kind to them.* "He who is devoid of wisdom despises his neighbor, but a man of understanding holds his peace" (Proverbs 11:12).

10. *Seek God's wisdom, not the world's.* "You are in Christ Jesus, who became for us wisdom from God" (1 Corinthians 1:3); "Has not God made foolish the wisdom of this world?" (1 Corinthians 1:20).

Ten Reasons to Ask God for Wisdom

1. *To enjoy a long life.* "Length of days is in her right hand, in her left hand riches and honor" (Proverbs 3:16). (The words "she" and "her" in all of the Proverbs listed in this section refer to wisdom.)

2. *To have a good life.* "Her ways are ways of pleasantness, and all her paths are peace" (Proverbs 3:17).

3. *To enjoy a life of happiness.* "She is a tree of life to those who take hold of her, and happy are all who retain her" (Proverbs 3:18).

4. *To be protected from danger.* "Then you will walk safely in your way, and your foot will not stumble" (Proverbs 3:23).

5. *To sleep without fear at night.* "When you lie down, you will not be afraid; yes, you will lie down and your sleep will be sweet" (Proverbs 3:24).

6. *To have confidence.* "For the LORD will be your confidence, and will keep your foot from being caught" (Proverbs 3:26).

7. *To be secure.* "Do not forsake her, and she will preserve you; love her, and she will keep you…When you walk, your steps will not be hindered, and when you run, you will not stumble" (Proverbs 4:6,12).

8. *To receive recognition in life.* "Exalt her, and she will promote you; she will bring you honor, when you embrace her" (Proverbs 4:8).

9. *To be protected from evil.* "When wisdom enters your heart, and knowledge is pleasant to your soul, discretion will preserve you; understanding will keep you, to deliver you from the way of evil, from the man who speaks perverse things" (Proverbs 2:10-12).

10. *To have understanding and knowledge.* "A wise man will hear and increase learning, and a man of understanding will attain wise counsel" (Proverbs 1:5).

Always Seek God's Counsel

Always ask God about things before you ask anyone else. I don't mean that you can't take advice from trustworthy people. I'm saying that before you go to them, ask God what you should do. Then pray that the person you are going to will have wisdom and knowledge to impart to you. Ask God to show you if you are receiving advice or guidance from a source that is not wise. Ask Him to lead you away from ungodly counsel and direct you to people who have godly wisdom. Before you make any decision, even to go someplace with someone, ask God for His wisdom about it.

My Prayer to God

Lord, I pray for comfort in trying times. I know You will work everything out, but sometimes it's hard to believe. I also pray for strength to resist temptation. I don't work very hard at that, but I know You're working in that area of my life.

(Age 15)

I Prayed and God Answered

My sister needed healing, so I prayed every night for God to heal her. Eventually doctors found a way to help her.

(Age 13)

If you make it a habit to always ask God for wisdom, then when you have to make quick decisions with no time to ask anyone anything, you will make a wise one because of the wisdom God has placed in you.

Just out of curiosity, I went down to the beach that day and swam out in the water to one of those shallow plateaus I had been observing from the balcony. I walked around on top of it to see exactly how much of the deep water could be determined from that close up. Because I had the advantage of knowing there was a steep drop-off on one side, I confidently walked toward the edge. Suddenly the whole edge collapsed and I fell in just as I'd seen other swimmers do. I realized that even when you think you know something, you still can't get smug about it. None of us should be too prideful to ask God for His wisdom and counsel, because He is the only one who knows the whole truth.

Prayer Power

Lord, I pray that You would give me wisdom in everything I do. I know wisdom is better than gold and understanding better than silver (Proverbs 16:16), so make me rich in wisdom and wealthy in understanding. Increase my wisdom and knowledge so I can see Your truth in every situation. Give me discernment for each decision I make.

Lord, help me to always seek godly counsel and not look to the world and people who don't know You for answers. Thank You, Lord, that "You will show me the path of life" (Psalm 16:7-11).

Help me to know and understand Your Word so I can get it into my soul and my heart. Lord, You have said that whoever "trusts in his own heart is a fool, but whoever walks wisely will be delivered" (Proverbs 28:26). I don't want to trust my own heart. I want to trust Your Word and Your instruction so that I can walk wisely and never do ignorant or stupid things. Make me a wise person.

Give me the wisdom, knowledge, understanding, direction, and discernment I need to keep me away from the plans of evil so that I will walk safely and not stumble (Proverbs 2:10-13). Lord, I know that in You "are hidden all the treasures of wisdom and knowledge" (Colossians 2:3). Help me to discover those treasures. In Jesus' name I pray.

WORD POWER

The fear of the LORD is the beginning of wisdom, and the knowledge of the Holy One is understanding. For by me your days will be multiplied, and years of life will be added to you.

PROVERBS 9:10-11

The mouth of the righteous speaks wisdom, and his tongue talks of justice. The law of his God is in his heart; none of his steps shall slide.

PSALM 37:30-31

If you cry out for discernment, and lift up your voice for understanding, if you seek her as silver, and search for her as for hidden treasures; then you will understand the fear of the LORD, and find the knowledge of God. For the LORD gives wisdom; from His mouth come knowledge and understanding.

PROVERBS 2:3-6

GIVING IT SOME FURTHER THOUGHT

1 I think it is more important to seek the wisdom of God than the wisdom of the world because:

2 The things I most need wisdom about at this time are: (Write this out as a prayer to God asking Him for the wisdom you need for these things.)

3 If the fear of the Lord is where wisdom begins in our life, write out a prayer to God telling Him how much you love and reverence Him. Ask Him to make you a wise person so that every decision you make is a wise one.

chapter 13

LORD, HELP ME

Get Rid of Negative Emotions

I USED TO THINK BEING ANXIOUS, DEPRESSED, and fearful was something I had to live with. I thought, *This is just the way I am, and there is nothing I can do about it.* But when I came to know the Lord and started living His way, I began to see that *all things* are possible to anyone who believes and obeys God. It's even possible to live without negative emotions. God will lift them off of us if we ask Him to. But we have to pray.

Have you ever felt as though God has forsaken you? Or that He is not listening to your prayers? Well, if you have, you're not alone. In fact, you're in very good company. Not only do millions of other people feel that way right now, but Jesus felt that way at one time too. At the lowest point in His life, Jesus said, "My God, My God, why have You forsaken Me?" (Matthew 27:46).

We all go through difficult times. Times when we feel alone and abandoned. But the truth is we aren't. God is with us during those times to get us through. We just have to call upon Him. In the midst of difficult times we can resist being controlled by negative emotions by praying, by knowing the truth of what God's Word says about them, and by taking the following steps.

Nine Ways to Get Free of Negative Emotions

1. *Refuse to be anxious about anything, knowing that God is in control of your life when you ask Him to be.* No matter what problems you have, Jesus has overcome them. "In the world you will have tribulation; but be of good cheer, I have overcome the world" (John 16:33). We can find freedom from anxiety just by spending time with God. "In the multitude of my anxieties within me, Your comforts delight my soul" (Psalm 94:19).

   When you are anxious, it means you aren't trusting God to take care of you. I know that trusting God to take care of everything is easier said than done. But God will prove to you that He is faithful to help you if you will go to Him for everything. "Do not seek what you should eat or what you should drink, nor have an anxious mind. For all these things the nations of the world seek after, and your Father knows that you need these things. But seek the kingdom of God, and all these things shall be added to you" (Luke 12:29-31). God says we don't need to be anxious about *anything*; we just need to pray about *everything.* And that is something you can do.

2. *Refuse to be ruled by anger.* Anger is a trap waiting for you to fall into. When you allow anger to rule your thoughts and actions,

I Feel Most Like Praying When:

- Something bad has happened
- I am struggling with something
- I feel sad and confused
- I'm happy
- I'm upset and need help

(Ages 13-15)

it causes you to do or say things you will one day regret. And it shuts off all God has for you the way pressure on a hose shuts off water flow. I've seen it happen countless times with people. Just when God is moving in their lives in a powerful way, they give in to anger and completely shut Him off. When we give anger a home in our souls, we open the door to sin and the devil. "'Be angry, and do not sin': do not let the sun go down on your wrath, nor give place to the devil" (Ephesians 4:26-27). An angry person upsets everyone around them, and they make serious mistakes as a result. "An angry man stirs up strife, and a furious man abounds in transgression" (Proverbs 29:22).

> **I Prayed and God Answered**
> I prayed my father's eyes would be opened to his neglect of his family. God answered that in a major way.
> (Age 16)

How many people have become violent and destroyed their lives and the lives of others because of their uncontrolled anger? How many angry people destroy their relationships and their families and sacrifice the destiny God has for them? Only foolish people are quick to get angry. People with wisdom don't want to pay the price. "Do not hasten in your spirit to be angry, for anger rests in the bosom of fools" (Ecclesiastes 7:9). Ask God to keep you free from anger so you can remain in the flow of all He has for you.

3. *Refuse to be dissatisfied and always complaining.* It's easy to constantly focus on the negative and look for everything that's wrong with your life. But that causes you to have constant unrest and you are never at peace. It not only makes *you* miserable, but it makes *everyone around you* miserable too. There is nothing wrong with wanting things to be different when they need to be, but when that attitude becomes a way of life, you sacrifice your peace.

Whenever you feel dissatisfied with your circumstances, remember that the apostle Paul said, "I have learned in whatever state I am, to be content" (Philippians 4:11). That kind of attitude takes faith. Faith to believe God is in control of your life. Faith to believe He loves you and knows what is best for you. Faith to believe His timing is perfect.

God promises, "There remains therefore a rest for the people of God" (Hebrews 4:9). That means it is possible to find contentment, rest, peace, and joy in any situation. One of the best Scriptures to memorize is "I can do all things through Christ who strengthens me" (Philippians 4:13). That means you can get through anything, even times of dissatisfaction and misery, because Jesus will enable you to.

4. *Refuse to be envious of what other people have.* Nothing good comes out of being envious of another person. When you focus on someone else and what *they* have, instead of on the Lord and what *He* has, a covetous spirit comes to confuse you and make your life miserable. "For where envy and self-seeking exist, confusion and every evil thing are there" (James 3:16).

Don't allow yourself to entertain thoughts like, *If only I had her hair…her face…her body…her clothes…his talent…his strength…her gifts…his wealth…her popularity.* Focus your thoughts toward Jesus instead. Think about *His* beauty, *His* wealth, *His* talents, *His* nature, *His* provision, *His* help, and *His* power. Thank Him for the rich inheritance you have in *Him*, and tell Him you can't wait to experience it all.

Covetousness started when Cain wanted what Abel had, and he killed him for it. But Cain suffered the rest of his life as a result. "Where there are envy, strife, and divisions among you, are you not carnal and behaving like mere men?" (1 Corinthians 3:3). We don't want to suffer for the rest of our lives because of envy. "A sound heart is life to the body, but envy is rottenness to the bones" (Proverbs 14:30). Pray that God's love would be manifested in you and through you at all times. "Love suffers long and is kind; love does not envy" (1 Corinthians 13:4).

5. *Refuse to allow depression to rule your life.* Of all negative emotions, I believe depression is the one we most readily accept as part of our lives. Many people live with depression without even realizing it because it feels so familiar. But God doesn't want us to accept this as a way of life.

My Prayer to God
Lord, help me to have faith that You are always with me.
(Age 17)

I am not talking about clinical depression that is due to an imbalance in the body and requires medicine to make it right. If you need medicine, take it. I am talking about a wounding of the soul that requires the healing touch of the Lord and the knowledge of the truth of God's Word to set you free. Feeling bad about yourself or your life, and feeling hopeless because you see no way around the things that bother you, can make you depressed.

The good news is that God doesn't want you to live with those feelings. He wants you to have the joy of the Lord rise in your heart and chase away spirits of heaviness. "Depart from me, all you workers of iniquity; for the LORD has heard the voice of my weeping. The LORD has heard my supplication; the LORD will receive my prayer" (Psalm 6:8-9). God wants you to pray and ask Him to lift you out of depression. If you are experiencing depression, don't tolerate it for even one moment longer.

6. *Refuse to be bitter about anything.* Bitterness burns away your body and soul the way acid eats skin. When a root of bitterness takes hold in your heart, it grows and cuts off the blessings of

God. "For I see that you are poisoned by bitterness and bound by iniquity" (Acts 8:23).

When you constantly have thoughts such as, *I can never forget what that person did to me; I should have won that award and not that other person,* then you have bitterness growing in you like a cancer. But if you can identify those thoughts right when they first start to take hold in your mind, and refuse to give them a place to dwell in your heart, then they cannot take root and grow.

When we are bitter, we are hostile, resentful, hateful, or antagonistic toward someone or something. Ask God to help you identify and resist bitterness in you. "Looking diligently lest anyone fall short of the grace of God; lest any root of bitterness springing up cause trouble, and by this many become defiled" (Hebrews 12:15). Pray for God to set you free from bitterness and ask Him to give you a spirit of thanksgiving and praise. That will crowd out anything in your heart that is not of Him.

7. *Refuse to live with feelings of rejection.* Many people who have felt rejected in their past for one reason or another live in fear of being rejected now and in the future. They *expect* to be rejected, so they read rejection into other people's words and actions. This causes them to always be hurt, afraid, angry, or bitter. It makes them oversensitive to the comments and actions of others. It drives the people around them crazy. In other words, their fear of rejection causes the very rejection they feared. It becomes an endless cycle. If you have ever felt that way, remember that God has not rejected you. He accepted you before you ever knew Him. You can't make everyone love you, but God loves you, and when you make Him the center of your life, He will give you favor with other people.

8. *Refuse to be hopeless about anything, no matter how hopeless it may seem.* Hopelessness is a slow killer that will eventually affect the health of your body and soul. But when you deliberately choose to put your hope in the Lord, He will take your hopelessness away. Just as we can choose what to wear each day, we can also choose to put our hope in God. We can guard our soul. "Thorns and snares are in the way of the perverse; he who guards his soul will be far from them" (Proverbs 22:5).

Hopelessness is death to our souls. Refuse to live with it. No matter how bad things appear to get in your life, because of the Lord you always have hope. He can do the impossible when you pray. He can do things you can't even dream of. He can find a way out of something that you can't see. Ask Him to give you hope for your future and an attitude of gratefulness every day of your life.

> **My Prayer to God**
> Lord, please be with me. I'm so scared and I don't know what to do. I feel like I'm completely alone and I need to know that You are with me. Please make me feel safe and give me comfort. Be my fortress; be my protector. Take away my fear and let me not be paralyzed by it so that I may live my life for You. I love You more than anything and I know Your perfect love casts out all fear.
> (Age 16)

9. *Refuse to let fear rule your life.* I have been afraid of many things in my life, but God has set me free of them all. I have been set free from the fear of dying, starving, failing, flying, accidents, knives, getting lost, being abandoned, getting sick, being injured, the dark, people's opinions, and being rejected, just to name a few. Some of those fears went away when I prayed about them specifically. Others went away as I learned to walk with the Lord and spend time in His presence.

God does not want us to live in fear. Fear does not come from Him. It's the world that teaches us to fear. The things we see in movies, videos, newspapers, books, and on television make us afraid. The things we hear people say and see them do cause us to have fear. The enemy can make us afraid of everything and wear us down with fear of what *could* happen. But we don't have to be tormented by fear.

One of the most common types of fear is the fear of what people think. We fear being rejected by them. It's a trap we can fall into without even realizing it. In order to protect ourselves from it, we have to care more about what God says than what anyone else says. We must look to Him for approval and acceptance and not to other people. If God does not have first place in our hearts, then we will be constantly fearing man. "The fear of man brings a snare, but whoever trusts in the LORD shall be safe" (Proverbs 29:25).

God wants to set us free from all fear. The Bible says that "there is no fear in love; but perfect love casts out fear (1 John 4:18). The only love that is perfect is the love of God. The way you get perfected in His love is to draw close to Him and let Him fill you with His love. When you do, He will deliver you from all fear.

Some of the ways to get rid of fear are to watch what you allow into your mind, pray often, praise God frequently; and read the Word of God. So many times in my life when I was afraid, I found that all fear left me just from reading the Bible or speaking some Bible verses like "God has not given us a spirit of fear, but of power and of love and of a sound mind" (2 Timothy 1:7).

God wants you to walk with Him and talk with Him and

have the kind of relationship with Him where He shares Himself with you and tells you things you didn't know before and wouldn't know unless He revealed them to you. When you get close enough to Him, all your fear will be gone.

Negative emotions reveal that we have doubt inside of us. If we completely trust God in our life, what do we have to be anxious about? Each one of us is susceptible to having negative emotions at some time, so don't feel bad if you have them. But don't live with them either. Refuse to allow the ugliness of negative emotions to mar the beauty of the life God has for you.

I Prayed and God Answered

I struggled with low self-esteem. I prayed about that and asked God to give me the desire to know Him better. He revealed Himself to me and used that situation to change me so I feel better about myself and my life now.

(Age 18)

Prayer Power

Lord, I pray that You will give me the strength to resist negative emotions such as anxiety, anger, dissatisfaction, envy, depression, bitterness, rejection, hopelessness, and fear. Rescue me when "my spirit is overwhelmed within me; my heart within me is distressed" (Psalm 143:4). I refuse to let my life be brought down by negative emotions because I know You have a better quality of life for me than that. When I am tempted to give in to these feelings, help me to remember all that is true about You.

You have said in Your Word that by our patience we can possess our souls (Luke 21:19). Give me the patience and understanding to be in control of my emotions. Help me to keep my "heart with all diligence," for I know that "out of it spring the issues of life" (Proverbs 4:23). Help me to not be insecure and focused on myself. Help me focus on You and other people. Help me not be oversensitive to myself, but rather be sensitive to the needs of other people. Thank You, Lord, that in my distress I can call on You. And when I pray to You, Lord, You will hear my voice and answer me (Psalm 18:6). May the joy of knowing You fill my heart at all times so I can live in Your joy and peace. In Jesus' name I pray.

WORD POWER

Be anxious for nothing, but in everything by prayer and supplication, with thanksgiving, let your requests be made known to God; and the peace of God, which surpasses all understanding, will guard your hearts and minds through Christ Jesus.

PHILIPPIANS 4:6-7

Come to Me, all you who labor and are heavy laden, and I will give you rest. Take My yoke upon you and learn from Me, for I am gentle and lowly in heart, and you will find rest for your souls. For My yoke is easy and My burden is light.

MATTHEW 11:28-30

The righteous cry out, and the LORD hears, and delivers them out of all their troubles. The LORD is near to those who have a broken heart, and saves such as have a contrite spirit.

PSALM 34:17-18

1

List the negative emotions you struggle with most and why you think you have them. Write out a prayer asking God to help you be completely free of all negative emotions, especially the ones you struggle with most.

2

What changes in you or your circumstances would you most like to see God make? Write your answer out as a prayer to God asking Him to make those changes.

3

Do you ever fear being rejected? Write out a prayer asking God to set you free from fear of the opinions of others.

chapter 14

"LORD, HELP ME" Resist Temptation

EVERYBODY IS TEMPTED BY SOMETHING. When we are tempted, we are drawn toward something we know is wrong. Being tempted doesn't mean anything is wrong with *you*. We all have fleshly thoughts sometimes. And we all have an enemy who tempts us to take *action* on those thoughts so he can ruin our lives and keep us from all that God has for us.

King David was tempted. When he took action on it, temptation nearly ruined his life. He was a young man with everything going for him. He had good looks, musical talent, courage, wealth, prominence, authority, a good family, and God's favor. Yet he fell into temptation and had to commit sin on top of sin trying to cover it up. He obviously had too much time on his hands, and he wasn't where he was supposed to be. He was out on the roof of his palace watching the woman next door take a bath instead of going to war with his men the way other kings did. His biggest mistake was not that he was exposed to temptation, for that can happen to anyone, but that he didn't turn away from it and run to God in repentance immediately.

I Pray for Others When:
- They feel down
- I sense danger lurking
- I see potential in them
- They are lonely
- They are not living right

(Ages 16-19)

He stayed and stared. He thought and schemed. He let his lust rule him instead of his God. He had an affair with this married woman, Bathsheba, while her husband was away at war. When she became pregnant, David had her husband murdered in order to cover up the affair. As a result of his succumbing to temptation, he became a murderer and an adulterer and ended up paying for it for the rest of his life—even to the point of seeing the death of two of his own sons.

Temptation happened to Jesus too. But He did the *right* thing and David did not. Jesus stood strong in the Word of God and David forgot about it.

I have seen far too many people sacrifice their lives by giving in to temptation. There are many kinds of temptation, such as lying, cheating, stealing, taking drugs, breaking the law, and disobeying the rules. The one that seems to trip up most people most often is sexual temptation. I have seen talented people succumb to sexual temptation and forfeit the promising life God had for them. They fell like meteors and burned themselves out when they could have been a shining star today.

I Prayed and God Answered
I asked God to provide money to go to a church retreat and He did.

(Age 18)

When people fall into sex sins of any kind, even when they

repent and receive God's forgiveness, they lose what *could* have been if this sin had never happened. David was forgiven and restored, but he lost the thing he loved most—his son—and his reign was marred from that point on with one disaster after another, including the death of another son and many family members. God still loved him, but his sin had consequences. People don't realize how great the consequences are when they give in to sexual temptation.

I Believe in Prayer Because:

- It moves mountains and does miracles
- God gives me strength when I pray
- God is faithful to answer my prayers
- It makes people change
- It is powerful and life-changing

(Ages 16-19)

If you ever find yourself being attracted to something or someone in a way that isn't pleasing to God, confess it immediately and ask Him to set you free from it. Don't wait a minute. Then tell Satan that you recognize his plan to destroy your life and separate you from all God has for you and you are not going to allow him to do it. Don't stop praying about it until the temptation is gone. "Watch and pray, lest you enter into temptation. The spirit indeed is willing, but the flesh is weak" (Matthew 26:41).

Six Things to Remember About Temptation

1. *Who:* Temptation can happen to anyone. No matter how spiritual and solid you think you are, you can fall into temptation. The people I have seen who fell the hardest were those who were prideful about what good Christians they were. They bragged about their spiritual strength and godliness, and their pride kept them from seeing the truth until it was too late.

2. *What:* You can be tempted by anything. The most common temptation today is sexual because the opportunity for it is everywhere and it is so accepted by our culture. But there are

other kinds of temptation, such as pornography, occult practices, and the unhealthy need for recognition, admiration, money, and power. "Each one is tempted when he is drawn away by his own desires and enticed. Then, when desire has conceived, it gives birth to sin; and sin, when it is full-grown, brings forth death. Do not be deceived" (James 1:14-16). The enemy will tempt you in the way you are most susceptible. Whenever anything tempts you, ask God to give you the strength to resist it. Guard your vulnerable areas with prayer.

3. *When:* Temptation can happen anytime and often when you least expect it. When it does happen, the danger is in thinking you can handle it alone. It's best to take it to God and confess it immediately, and then find someone trustworthy to pray with you about it. Don't think temptation will just pass. *The pull is too powerful. The risk is too great.* Treat it as a serious threat no matter when it happens.

4. *Where*: Temptation can happen anywhere. In church, in school, at work, at home, on a bus or a plane. It will happen in the place you least expect it. Wherever it is, separate yourself from it immediately. If chocolate tempts you, don't hang out in the candy store. The smell of it will drive you crazy and weaken your resistance. If a certain person tempts you to do things you know you shouldn't, don't be around him or her. Or if you must be with them, don't be alone. Separate yourself from the temptation and ask God to kill that lust in you. He will!

5. *Why:* The reason the enemy tempts you is because he knows of the great things God wants to do in your life, and he thinks you are dumb enough to give it all up for a few moments of worldly pleasure. He knows that not only do you stand to lose from it, but *other people* will be hurt by your sin as well. When you recognize the trap he is setting for you, decide right then

that you are not going to fall into it and allow him to destroy your life.

6. *How:* You have to remember that no matter how you are being tempted, it is a setup by the enemy intended to bring you down. He will find your greatest weakness, need, or insecurity and try to lure you with whatever you are most easily attracted to. This is the best reason to get rid of your insecurities and become a whole person. It eliminates one of the ways the enemy has access to your life. For example, you may be tempted to do something wrong in order to be liked or accepted. But if you know who you are in the Lord, you won't fall for it.

Temptation Evasion

The best way to avoid falling into temptation is to pray about it *before* it happens. After temptation presents itself, resisting it becomes much more difficult. Jesus taught us to pray, "Do not lead us into temptation, but deliver us from the evil one" (Matthew 6:13). That may sound to you like God is the one tempting us, but He doesn't do that. We are tempted by the enemy, and we are tempted by what our flesh wants.

God tells us that we are to "stand fast therefore in the liberty by which Christ has made us free, and do not be entangled again with a yoke of bondage" (Galatians 5:1). We can call on the name of the Lord, "for in that He Himself has suffered, being tempted, He is able to aid those who are tempted" (Hebrews 2:18). Don't ever think you are immune to temptation. Jesus instructed His own disciples to

I Prayed and God Answered
I was going through a depression and my friends invited me to church and talked to me about God. I prayed for God to come into my heart and never leave me. And now I feel better about life.
(Age 18)

My Prayer to God
Lord, please remove any temptation from my heart and mind. Take it and destroy it completely.
(Age 14)

"rise and pray, lest you enter into temptation" (Luke 22:46). You must do that too.

With regard to sexual temptation, ask God to keep you pure and untarnished. If you have already fallen in this area, ask God to make this day a new beginning for you. He will do that. There comes a time in all of our lives when we are desperate to know that God is close and that He hears our prayers and will answer. We won't have time to *get* right with God; we will have to already *be* right with God. Now is the time to start living pure lives if we want to see our prayers answered in the future.

Jesus' temptation happened just before the greatest breakthrough in His life. It will happen before the greatest breakthrough in yours too. Be ready for it. And remember that no matter how great the temptation is you face, "He who is *in you* is greater than he who is in the world" (1 John 4:4). Because of Jesus in you, you have the power to overcome temptation.

Prayer Power

Lord, make me strong so I don't fall into any traps of the enemy. Do not allow me to be led into temptation, but deliver me from the evil one and his plans for my downfall. The area I am most concerned about is (name any area where you might be tempted). In the name of Jesus, I break any hold temptation has on me. Help me to resist anything that would tempt me away from all You have for me.

I pray that I will have no secret thoughts where I entertain ungodly desires to do or say something I shouldn't. I pray that I will have no secret life where I do things I would be ashamed to have others see. Don't allow the enemy to sneak up on my blind side and take me by surprise.

Lord, I know You have called me to purity. Help me to "cling to what is good" (Romans 12:9) and keep myself pure (1 Timothy 5:22). Help me to separate myself from all that is not of You, and not have confusion about this. Give me discernment to recognize anything in my life that is worthless so I can get rid of it. Set me free from any weakness that could lead me away from all You have for me (Psalm 145:18-19). Thank You that You know "how to deliver the godly out of temptations" (2 Peter 2:9). Thank You for delivering me out of all temptation and keeping it far from me. In Jesus' name I pray.

WORD POWER

Blessed is the man who endures temptation; for when he has been approved, he will receive the crown of life which the Lord has promised to those who love Him.

JAMES 1:12

No temptation has overtaken you except such as is common to man; but God is faithful, who will not allow you to be tempted beyond what you are able, but with the temptation will also make the way of escape, that you may be able to bear it.

1 CORINTHIANS 10:13

Therefore let him who thinks he stands take heed lest he fall.

1 CORINTHIANS 10:12

1 What are the greatest temptations facing you in your life today at school, at home, at work, or wherever you go? What do you need to do to avoid these temptations?

2 Write out your own prayer asking God to keep you away from the things that tempt you to do what isn't right in the sight of God. Ask Him to forgive you for any time when you have given in.

3 Describe a time when God kept you from falling into temptation. What are the reasons you think that resisting temptation is good for your future?

chapter 15

"Lord, Help Me"

Be Strong When Bad Things Happen

HAVE YOU EVER TAKEN OFF IN AN AIRPLANE on a cloudy, gray, dreary, rainy day? Every time I have done that I'm always amazed at how we can fly right up through dark, wet clouds that are so thick we can't see one thing out the window. And then suddenly we rise above it all and have the ability to see for miles. Up there the sky is sunny, clear, and blue. I keep forgetting that no matter how bad the weather gets down below, it's possible to rise above the storm to a place where everything is fine.

Our spiritual and emotional lives are like that too. Did you know that when the dark clouds of trial, trouble, struggle, grief, or suffering roll into our lives and settle on us so thick and dark that we can barely see ahead of us, there is a place of light, calm, and peace that we can rise to? If we take God's hand in prayer in those

The Hardest Thing About Prayer Is:

- Expressing what I'm feeling
- Knowing what to say
- Feeling God's presence
- Knowing there is so much to pray about
- Not knowing if God really cares

  (Ages 16-19)

difficult times, He will lift us up above our circumstances to the place of comfort He has for us.

One of my favorite names for the Holy Spirit is the Comforter (John 14:26 ASV). Just as we don't have to beg the sun for light, we don't have to beg the Holy Spirit for comfort. He *is* comfort. Whenever you are going through a bad time, pray that the Holy Spirit will give you a greater sense of His comfort in it. That's something He *wants* to do. Jesus said, "Blessed are those who mourn, for they shall be comforted (Matthew 5:4). It's a done deal.

Tough times happen to all of us at one time or another. Pain and loss are a part of life. Everyone will have someone they care about die, or move away, or get divorced. Everyone will lose something or someone at sometime someday. Everyone will experience disappointment, discouragement, or some kind of disaster. There are many different reasons why these things happen, but no matter what happens, God is always there to bring good out of it when we invite Him to. If you are able to understand the possible reasons for your suffering, it will help you to overcome your pain and see your faith grow in the midst of it.

Four Good Reasons for Bad Times

1. *Sometimes difficult things happen to us so that the glory and power of God can be revealed in and through us.* When Jesus passed by a man who was born blind, His disciples asked Him if the man's blindness was because he had sinned or because his parents had sinned. Jesus replied, "Neither this man nor his parents sinned, but that the works of God should be revealed

I Pray for Others When:
- They are sick or injured
- They are not living right
- They are on my heart
- They don't know the Lord
- They are in need
  (Ages 16-19)

in him" (John 9:3). You may not be able to understand why certain things are happening to you at the time, and you may never know why you have to go through them until you go to be with the Lord, but when you turn to God in the midst of a difficult situation, He will bring good out of it and that gives people hope. They feel that God might do the same for *them*. When they see your strength in the middle of what is happening, it gives them courage to face their own problems.

2. *Sometimes God allows us to go through difficult times in order to make us into better people.* The Bible says, "Since Christ suffered for us in the flesh, arm yourselves also with the same mind, for he who has suffered in the flesh has ceased from sin" (1 Peter 4:1). This means our suffering during difficult times will burn sin and selfishness out of our lives. God allows suffering to happen so that we will learn to live for *Him* and not for ourselves. So that we will pursue *His* will and not our own. It's not pleasant at the time, but God wants us to let go of everything else and cling to what is most important in life—Him. When you hang on to Him through the tough times, He will give you strength.

3. *Sometimes our misery is caused by God disciplining us.* It never feels good to be disciplined, but we always learn something important from it. It saves our lives. "No chastening seems to be joyful for the present, but painful; nevertheless, afterward it yields the peaceable fruit of righteousness to those who have been trained by it" (Hebrews 12:11). God is always trying to teach us something in the difficult times we go through. "Do

I Prayed and God Answered

My grandfather and I prayed for my grandma's migraines and they went away.

(Age 16)

not despise the chastening of the LORD, nor be discouraged when you are rebuked by Him; for whom the LORD loves He chastens, and scourges every son whom He receives" (Hebrews 12:5-6). When you go through bad times, ask God to show you what you need to see in the situation. Whatever He teaches you will make you stronger.

4. *Sometimes the sorrow, sadness, grief, or pain of difficult times is entirely the work of the enemy.* It's not your fault or anyone else's. The enemy is always wanting to make you miserable and destroy your life. But God wants you to call on Him so He can deliver you from the enemy. God wants you to walk with Him in faith as He leads you through the tough times. He wants you to trust Him in the middle of them. No one wants to hear about how good pain and suffering are for them. When you're experiencing trouble, tragedy, loss, devastation, or disappointment, you can't think beyond the fact that you are hurting and you want to be free of the pain. But you must remember that if you will pray and praise God in the middle of your pain, He will defeat the enemy for you and bring good out of it that you can't even imagine.

Being a Comforter Yourself

In some translations of the Bible, the Holy Spirit is called the Helper. Jesus said, "I will pray the Father, and He will give you another Helper, that He may abide with you forever—the Spirit of truth" (John 14:16-17). When we turn to the Holy Spirit for help and comfort, He will not only give us aid, but He will give us more of His presence than we have ever had before (Matthew 5:4).

When my best friend died I was devastated with grief. We had been friends for years and I didn't know how I could live without her. The day after the funeral brought the worst pain of all, because that was the day reality set in and it hit me hard that I would never see her again. But I went to God that day for comfort and asked Him to take away my grief and get me through that time. I felt Him do that.

One of the things I learned through that time was how to comfort someone else who is going through that same kind of loss. I learned how important it is to be there for them and just listen. I learned how to tell them about the comfort of the Lord. I wouldn't have known all that if I hadn't gone through it myself. One of the things God teaches us in tough times is how to not only *receive* His comfort, but how we can *give* comfort to others when they are going through a similar situation. Suffering increases your compassion for the sufferings of others.

Another thing I learned was that you can have peace and joy in the middle of the most difficult and miserable situation. That's because joy comes from the Lord. That doesn't mean you suddenly become delusional or happy about the difficulty. It means that you know God is in charge of your life, and He will not only get you through it, but there will be something good that comes out of it.

When bad things happen, turn to God in prayer, and He will either take your pain away, change the situation, help you get through it, or enable you rise above it. If you continue to live in the

My Prayer to God
Lord, I come to You knowing that You are the answer to all my struggles. You always have a solution. I ask You to bless my future. Let everything I do be pleasing to You. No matter where my future takes me, help me to guard my heart so that I am always owned by You.
(Age 15)

presence of the Lord, His glory will be revealed in you. Others will see it, and it will give them hope.

Prayer Power

Lord, help me to remember that no matter what bad times I go through, or what kind of dark clouds settle on my life, You are my Comforter. Only You can lift me above the storm and into Your presence. Only You can take whatever loss I experience and fill that empty place with good. Only You can take the burden of my grief and pain and bring something positive out of it. "Hear me when I call, O God of my righteousness! You have relieved me in my distress; have mercy on me, and hear my prayer" (Psalm 4:1).

When I go through tough times, I pray that I will have a greater sense of Your presence with me. I want to grow stronger in these times and not weaker. I want to increase in faith and not be overcome with doubt. I want to have hope in the middle of them and not become hopeless. I want to stand strong in Your truth and not be swept away by my emotions.

Help me to remember to give thanks to You no matter what is happening because You are greater than anything I am facing. I know when I pass through the waters You will be with me and the river will not overflow me. When I walk through the fire I will not be burned, nor will the flame touch me (Isaiah 43:1-2). That's because You are a good God and have sent Your Holy Spirit to be my Comforter and Helper. Thank You that You will fill me with joy and peace so that I will "abound in hope by the power of the Holy Spirit" (Romans 15:13). In Jesus' name I pray.

WORD POWER

Beloved, do not think it strange concerning the fiery trial which is to try you, as though some strange thing happened to you; but rejoice to the extent that you partake of Christ's sufferings, that when His glory is revealed, you may also be glad with exceeding joy.

1 PETER 4:12-13

May the God of all grace, who called us to His eternal glory by Christ Jesus, after you have suffered a while, perfect, establish, strengthen, and settle you.

1 PETER 5:10

Count it all joy when you fall into various trials, knowing that the testing of your faith produces patience. But let patience have its perfect work, that you may be perfect and complete, lacking nothing.

JAMES 1:2-4

1 What was the toughest time you have gone through in the last two or three years? Did you sense the comfort of God during that time? Did you reach out to God in prayer to get you through it? What would you do differently next time? What would you do the same?

2 Write out a prayer asking God to be with you whenever you go through difficult times. Ask Him to help you turn to Him right away and not try to go through it alone.

3 What have you learned from going through hard times that has made you better able to help someone else going through their own hard time?

chapter 16

'LORD, HELP ME' Be Safe

WHILE I WAS WRITING THIS BOOK, I did my own personal survey among teenagers regarding their greatest concerns and what role prayer played in their lives. It was wonderful to talk to them and read what they wrote on the survey forms I had them fill out. Because I decided to make everything they revealed to me anonymous, they had the freedom to share honestly about the things they were experiencing and how they felt about it.

In this generation of teenagers, I found that most of you are very aware of what is going on in the world around you. You feel a lot of pressure to succeed, and you know the competition is intense. But you also have great hope that there is a good future ahead for you out there.

One of the most important things you have tremendous

I Feel Most Like Praying When:

- I am anxious
- I am driving to work
- I've been with unsaved friends
- I have a big test coming up
- I have a heavy burden on my heart

(Ages 16-19)

concerns about is your personal safety and the safety of those you care about. And for good reason. You watch television. You read magazines. You're on the Internet. You have, or at least have access to, a telephone or cell phone. You are plugged in and know that frightening things are going on in the world, and some of them are hitting way too close to home. Actually, you probably know more than you need to about what's going on, and it is unsettling to you. But there is a way to keep from having to live in fear about your own safety as well as the safety of others, and that is to pray about it. When you lift those concerns up to God every time you have them, and ask Him to protect you and all that you care about, you can live with greater peace about it.

Making Prayer Familiar Territory

I learned a long time ago to pray every day for my safety and the safety of my friends and family members. It always gave me peace to do it, and I know that God has protected us all because of it. Praying doesn't mean that nothing bad will ever happen, but even in the midst of things that do happen, you will see God's hand of protection.

I remember driving one time in my four-wheel-drive vehicle a few days after a big snowstorm. As I slowly approached a red light at a busy intersection, I put my foot on the brake, but nothing happened. I had hit a patch of black ice that was completely invisible to me. The intersection consisted of narrow two-lane highways crossing one another, with deep water-drainage ditches on either side. There were cars going both ways across the intersection in front of me, and I realized my car was entirely out of control and I couldn't stop.

"Jesus, help me," I prayed out loud. I tried my best to maintain control over the car and keep it from flipping over into one of the ditches on either side of me. In an effort to do that, however, I spun out in the center of the intersection. Cars dodged all around me as they tried to maintain control as well. One green car was headed directly toward me, and I don't even know how I

I Think of God As:
- My only Hope
- Omnipresent, always there
- A mighty King
- Someone who is close
- Too far away to hear me

(Ages 16-19)

missed hitting it, except to say that I was praying so strongly at the time that the hand of God must have intervened. It was miraculous that nothing happened to me or anyone else.

Before I left home that day, I had prayed specifically that God would keep me safe. There is no doubt in my mind that He answered that prayer. In those precarious moments, when your future is hanging in the balance, you want the confidence of knowing you have been communicating with your heavenly Father all along and He has His eye on you. These are the times, such as what

I experienced, when you need a prayer answered instantly. But in order to be sure that happens, you must be praying every day. God is a place of safety you can run to, but it helps if you are running to Him on a daily basis so that you are in familiar territory.

My Prayer to God
Lord, lead me in to Your will. Use me to accomplish things in this world and to do Your tasks, not mine.

(Age 13)

The Bible says, "In the fear of the LORD there is strong confidence, and His children will have a place of refuge. The fear of the LORD is a fountain of life, to turn one away from the snares of death"

(Proverbs 14:26-27). When we have our eyes on God, He keeps His eyes on us.

God Protects Us More Than We Know

Personally, I believe that our heavenly Father looks out for us and protects us from danger far more than we realize. We have no idea how many times we have just missed a dangerous situation and have been kept out of the way of something harmful. But this kind of protection is not something we can just take for granted. We have to pray about it.

Part of being protected by God has to do with obeying Him and living in His will. When we don't do either of those things, we can come out from under the umbrella of His covering over us. We are unable to hear His voice telling us which way to go and what to do. How many times would people have been spared from something disastrous if they had only asked God to show them the way and then followed His leading? If only they had been communicating more often with Him so that they could recognize His quiet voice speaking to their heart. If only they had taken the time to ask God for direction. If only they had been listening to God when He spoke to them through His Word or through an authority figure He had put in their life.

I Believe In Prayer Because:
- It makes people change
- It is powerful
- It can move mountains
- It changes situations
- It works

(Ages 13-15)

It is especially important to remember all this when you are driving. Always pray for safety when you get in a car. Don't take chances by not obeying all the rules of the road carefully. The price is way too high. Ask God to keep you alert and sensitive to what is going on in the cars around you. You can be the best driver and still get in an accident because of someone else's carelessness. If you do get into a small accident, let it be a lesson learned. The most cautious drivers I know are ones who have been in an accident and learned the hard way. Don't think for a moment that it can't happen to you. It can! So pray for God's protection whenever you drive.

Your prayers for protection over your school are also very important. Wherever you attend classes, ask God to pour out His Spirit on your school and protect it from any danger or evil. Pray for peace among the other students. Pray that any plans for evil will be exposed and thwarted.

Just remember that if there is ever anything that concerns you about your safety or the safety of others, let that be your cue to pray about it. Don't leave your life to chance in any way when you can cover it in prayer.

I Prayed and God Answered

I had a bad feeling about one of my friends who has an eating disorder. I prayed for her. I found out the next morning that she blacked out in her car and ran off the road into a ditch. God answered my prayer because she was okay.

(Age 16)

Prayer Power

Lord, I pray that You would always protect me wherever I go and keep me safe from any accidents, diseases, or evil influences. Keep me safe whenever I am driving or riding in a car with someone else. I want to be hidden in Your shadow from danger (Psalm 91:1). Help me to always hear Your voice leading and guiding me. Send Your angels to keep charge over me. (Psalm 91:12). Specifically, I pray for (name any area of special concern for your safety).

Lord, I look to You for my healing. Specifically I pray for (name any area where you need to be healed). I pray the same for my family and friends. Specifically I pray for (name the people who need healing). Thank You, Lord, that You are our Healer.

You, Lord, are my refuge and my strength and "a very present help in trouble." Therefore I will not be afraid. Protect me from violence and let no weapon be used against me (Isaiah 54:17). Thank You that You will not leave me in the hands of wicked people who would try to destroy me (Psalm 37:32-33). Protect me from the plans of evil people. Keep me from sudden danger. Thank You that "You alone, O LORD, make me dwell in safety" (Psalm 4:8). In Jesus' name I pray.

WORD POWER

Because you have made the LORD, who is my refuge, even the Most High, your dwelling place, no evil shall befall you, nor shall any plague come near your dwelling.

PSALM 91:9-10

No weapon formed against you shall prosper.

ISAIAH 54:17

He shall give His angels charge over you, to keep you in all your ways.

PSALM 91:11

1 Make a list of people you are most concerned about for their safety. Then say a prayer, naming each of these people and asking God to protect them. Don't forget yourself.

2 What things make you most afraid? Write them below as a prayer asking God to protect you from those things and set you free from any fear. (For example, "Lord, I am afraid of...")

3 When do you feel the most safe? Why? Thank God for those places of safety and peace.

chapter 17

"Lord, Help Me" Speak Words That Bring Life

WHEN I WAS 14, I INTRODUCED A NEIGHBOR boy to one of my girl-friends as "Fat Mike." All the other kids called him Fat Mike to distinguish him from the other Mikes who weren't as heavy. The moment I did that, however, I saw a hurt look in his eyes, and I realized that this was not a name he called himself. I felt very bad about that because I never intended to hurt him. In fact, I thought Mike was good-looking, and I didn't find his being on the heavy side unattractive at all. But he obviously did. I just thought this was a funny nickname he was okay with. He obviously wasn't. I was too ignorant at the time to realize no one feels good about a name like that. And I was also too embarrassed and immature to apologize. I hoped that by pretending the entire incident didn't happen that he would forget about it and everything would be fine.

The Hardest Thing About Prayer Is:

- Being able to praise God
- Not taking too long to do it
- Not knowing if God really cares
- Praying for myself
- Nothing's hard about it

(Ages 16-19)

I moved away from that neighborhood not long after that and never saw him again. I didn't think much about the incident until years later, after I became a believer. I wanted to be completely right with God and mend the past, so I asked the Lord to bring to my mind anything I needed to be forgiven of so I could confess it to Him. My mind was flooded with many memories of things I had done wrong, and one of them was my introduction of Mike. I felt terrible about my unintentionally cruel and thoughtless words and the damage they must have done. I couldn't believe that after all the times I had been hurt in my life by the callous comments of others, I had done the same thing to someone else. I asked God to forgive me for being so unloving, insensitive, and stupid.

If I could have found Mike and apologized to him in person, I would have. But I couldn't, so I tried to make it up to him by praying for him that God would bless his life in every way. I prayed that somehow the words I said would be erased from his memory, or at least they would lose their sting and he would be healed of any pain my comment must have caused him. I prayed he would be able to forgive me. I prayed I could forgive myself.

One of areas that can cause the greatest trouble in our lives is located on our face between the chin and the nose. With our mouth we can say things we shouldn't and end up hurting others and paying the consequences. I was paying the consequences for words I had said years ago.

We can't take our words back once we speak them. All we can do is apologize and hope to be forgiven by the person we hurt or insulted. The best way to make sure that what comes out of our mouth is good is to put thoughts in our heart that are good. The Bible says that "out of the abundance of the heart the mouth speaks" (Matthew 12:34). If we fill our heart with God's truth and God's love, that's what will come out.

I Feel Most Like Praying When:
- I'm depressed
- In the middle of the night
- I am tempted
- I feel God's presence
- I've just gotten out of church

(Ages 13-15)

Have you ever been around someone who complains all the time or speaks negatively about themselves and others? Isn't it exhausting? The Bible says we are to "do all things without complaining and disputing" (Philippians 2:14). If we complain, it reflects our lack of faith in God. It proves that we don't believe He is in charge and can take care of us. It suggests that we don't trust God will answer our prayers. It shows we are not praying. Being around people with such an obvious lack of faith is depleting.

Imagine if every time you opened your mouth you spoke words that were laced with healing, encouragement, comfort, wisdom, love, and truth. You would be the most popular person around. (Except with the complainers and negative thinkers, of course.) Talking that way all the time is hard to do on our own, but it's possible to do if you ask God to help you. It's dangerous to speak whatever comes into your mind—unless what comes into your mind is good. If you have your mind fixed on good things, and your heart is filled with good things, then the words of your mouth will reflect that.

Eight Good Things to Think About Daily

(From Philippians 4:8)

1. *Think about whatever things are true.* If you are thinking about

what is honest, genuine, authentic, sincere, faithful, accurate, and truthful, then you won't be saying anything false, incorrect, erroneous, deceitful, or untrue.

2. *Think about whatever things are noble.* If you are thinking about what is admirable, of high quality, excellent, magnanimous, superior, or honorable, then you won't be saying anything that is base, petty, mean, dishonorable, or low-minded.

3. *Think about whatever things are just.* If you are thinking about what is fair, reasonable, proper, lawful, right, correct, deserved, and honorable, then you won't be saying anything that is unjustified, biased, unreasonable, unlawful, or unfair.

4. *Think about whatever things are pure.* If you are thinking about what is clean, clear, spotless, chaste, undefiled, or untainted with evil, then you won't be saying anything that is inferior, tainted, adulterated, defiled, polluted, corrupted, unholy, or tarnished.

5. *Think about whatever things are lovely.* If you are thinking about what is pleasing, agreeable, charming, satisfying, or splendid, then you won't be saying anything that is unpleasant, offensive, disagreeable, revolting, unlovely, ominous, or ugly.

6. *Think about whatever things are of good report.* If you are thinking about what is admirable, winsome, worthwhile, recommended, positive, or worthy of repeating, then you won't be saying anything that is negative, discouraging, undesirable, or full of bad news, gossip, and rumor.

7. *Think about whatever things are virtuous.* If you are thinking about what is moral, ethical, upright, excellent, good, impressive, or conforming to high moral standards, then you won't

be saying anything that is depraved, unethical, licentious, bad, self-indulgent, dissipated, evil, or immoral.

8. *Think about whatever things are worthy of praise.* If you are thinking about what is admirable, commendable, valuable, acclaimed, applauded, glorified, exalted, honored, or approved of, then you won't be saying anything that is critical, condemning, disapproving, disparaging, denouncing, belittling, or depressing.

Five Things That Happen When a Wise Person Speaks

1. *When a wise person speaks, they give a reason for the hope they have within them.* The most important words we can speak are ones that explain our faith to someone who asks or to anyone who will listen. God says we must be able to give a reason for the hope we have within us (1 Peter 3:15). We have to pray that God will help us become wise enough and bold enough to clearly explain our faith in Him. We have to ask Him to help us tell others why we call Jesus our Messiah, why we can't live without the Holy Spirit, and why we choose to live God's way. And we must be able to do this in a manner that is loving and humble, otherwise we will alienate those whom God wants to draw to Himself. If the love of God is not in your heart, then it will not come out of your mouth. And what you say will not draw people to the Lord. It may, in fact, do the exact opposite.

2. *When a wise person speaks, they know that timing is important.* When things need to be said that are difficult for the hearer to receive, timing is everything. Certain words cannot be uttered with any success if the person listening is not open and ready to hear them. It's important to discern that, and the only way to know for certain when to speak and what to say is to pray for wisdom about that in advance. The Bible says that we are

not to be too hasty to speak (Proverbs **29:20**). A wise person knows they shouldn't share every single thought that comes into their head. "A fool vents all his feelings, but a wise man holds them back" (Proverbs **29:11**). You may have good things to say, but people aren't always ready to hear them. Only God knows for sure when someone is ready. Ask Him to show you.

3. *When a wise person speaks, they tell the truth.* When we don't speak the truth, we hurt others as well as ourselves.

"Therefore, putting away lying, 'Let each one of you speak the truth with his neighbor,' for we are members of one another" (Ephesians **4:25**). Lies hurt everyone. On the other hand, we can't run around speaking the truth without wisdom, sensitivity, and a sense of the Lord's timing. That hurts people. People don't want to hear every bit of truth about themselves every moment. It's too much for them. It's too much for us too. Sometimes it's better to say nothing and pray for God to show you when a person is ready to hear the truth. The truth you need to speak,

The Main Things I Pray About Are:
- That my food will be blessed at mealtimes
- That I will have courage
- That I will grow in my walk with God
- The my unsaved friends will know Jesus
- That I will have strength

(Ages 16-19)

especially about yourself and others, is *God's* truth. Don't speak negative things about yourself or anyone else because those kinds of words don't match up with the Word of God.

4. *When a wise person speaks, they don't talk too much.* We have to be careful that we don't spend more time talking than is necessary. The Bible says, "A fool's voice is known by his many words" (Ecclesiastes **5:3**). I always told my prayer groups that

we shouldn't spend more time talking about our prayer requests than we do praying about them. And we can't just spill words out of our mouth without giving thought to what we are saying. The Bible says we will give account of every idle word in the day of judgment (Matthew 12:36). This is a very scary thought. We must ask God to make us wise in the amount of talking we do.

5. *When a wise person speaks, their words are gracious.* We can't speak words that are mean, insensitive, harsh, coarse, rude, deceitful, offensive, or arrogant without reaping the consequences. With our words we will either build lives or we will tear them down. And that includes our own life. "The words of a wise man's mouth are gracious, but the lips of a fool shall swallow him up" (Ecclesiastes 10:12). Ask God to create in you a clean heart so filled with His Spirit, His love, and His truth that it will overflow love, truth, and healing in your speech. Ask Him to help you find words that speak life to those around you.

When I worked in the secular entertainment industry in Los Angeles, I heard the word "Jesus" a hundred times a day. But it was spoken as a curse word by people with no reverence, love, or understanding of who He is. It wasn't until I received Jesus that I realized exactly how much of a curse word that name was when it was used as profanity. Taking God's name in vain brings a curse on whoever uses it in that manner because it is breaking one of the Ten Commandments. "You shall not take the name of the LORD your God in vain, for the LORD will not hold him guiltless who takes His name in vain" (Exodus

I Prayed and God Answered

I prayed that I could talk to people at my school about God, and so far I have led 15 people at my school to the Lord.

(Age 13)

My Prayer to God
Lord, keep me pure. I pray also for my future spouse. Help us both to stay pure for each other until we marry.
(Age 13)

20:7). Using God's name as a curse word also violates God's *greatest* commandment, which is "You shall love the LORD your God with all your heart, with all your soul, with all your mind, and with all your strength" (Mark 12:30). No one who loves God uses His name in vain. However, this same word—Jesus—when spoken in love by someone who reverences Him, has great power in it. It has the power to save, deliver, heal, provide, protect, and so much more. Using it profanely shuts off these very things from our lives.

What you speak affects your life more than you know. When you bless others, God blesses you. Wise people know this and choose their words and timing carefully. Don't let any of the great things God wants to do in your future be cut off from you because of careless words you speak today.

Prayer Power

Lord, help me be a person who always speaks the truth and never lies. Help me to speak words that build people up and don't tear them down. Help me to speak life into the situations and people around me, and not death. Fill my heart each day with Your love and goodness so that it overflows from my mouth. Help me to speak only about things that are true, noble, just, pure, lovely, of good report, virtuous, and praiseworthy. "Let the words of my mouth and the meditation of my heart be acceptable in Your sight, O LORD, my strength and my Redeemer" (Psalm 19:14).

Your Word says that "the preparations of the heart belong to man, but the answer of the tongue is from the LORD" (Proverbs 16:1). Help me to prepare my heart by being in

Your Word. Fill my heart with Your love so that is what comes out in the words I speak. Convict my heart when I complain or speak negatively. Keep me from speaking words that hurt other people. Help me not to speak too quickly or too much. Show me when to speak and when not to. And when I do speak, give me words to say that will help people and make them feel good about themselves and their life. Give me words to explain my faith in a way that draws people to You. In Jesus' name I pray.

WORD POWER

He who would love life and see good days, let him refrain his tongue from evil, and his lips from speaking deceit.

1 PETER 3:10

The heart of the wise teaches his mouth, and adds learning to his lips.

PROVERBS 16:23

Pleasant words are like a honeycomb, sweetness to the soul and health to the bones.

PROVERBS 16:24

1 Has anyone ever spoken words to you that hurt your feelings or made you feel bad about yourself or your life? What was the most hurtful time you can remember? How does that memory affect the way you speak to others?

2 Have you ever spoken words to someone that may have hurt them or that you regret saying? If so, confess that to God and ask Him to help you apologize to that person.

3 Write out a prayer asking God to reveal to you any time you spoke words that hurt someone, or used language that wasn't pleasing to Him, that you are not even aware of. Write down what He shows you and ask Him to forgive you.

chapter 18

'LORD, HELP ME'

Have Faith for the Impossible

BEFORE I WAS A TEENAGER, SOMEONE gave me a small clear glass ball that looked like a large marble hanging from a gold chain. Inside the ball was the tiniest seed. A mustard seed. I thought at the time, *Why did they bother putting a seed in there so small I could hardly see it?* Obviously, I didn't get the point.

It wasn't until years later that I learned the significance of that little seed. Jesus said, "If you have faith as a mustard seed, you will say to this mountain, 'Move from here to there,' and it will move; and nothing will be impossible for you" (Matthew **17:20**). Since then I've thought a lot about how tiny that seed was. I decided if that's all the faith it takes to move a mountain, then surely I can come up with enough faith to move the mountains in my life.

Isn't it great that God can take the tiniest bit of faith we have and make it grow into something big when we act on it? The Bible

The Hardest Thing About Prayer Is:
- Waiting for God's timing
- Praying out loud in front of other people
- Praying about the bad things my friends are doing
- Not asking God to punish others
- Not knowing when God will answer

(Ages 16-19)

says that "God has dealt to each one a measure of faith" (Romans 12:3). That means He has already given us some faith to start with. But when we take *action* on our faith—step out and do something that takes faith on our part to do—God increases it.

Whether you realize it or not, you are living by faith every day. Each time you go to a doctor, you trust he is not going to kill you. When you buy medicine from the pharmacist, you believe he will fill your prescription correctly. When you go to a restaurant, you have faith the staff will not poison you. (Some restaurants require more faith than others.) How much more should we trust God?

How Great Things Happen

We have no idea what great things God wants to do through us if we will just step out in faith when He asks us to. That's why He lets us go through some difficult times. Times when we feel weak and vulnerable. He allows certain things to happen so that we will turn to Him and give Him our full attention. It's in those times, when we are forced to pray in greater faith, that our faith grows stronger. Jesus said, "According to your faith let it be to you" (Matthew 9:29). This could be a frightening thought, depending on the kind of faith we have. But there are things we can do to increase our faith.

One of the things you can do to increase your faith is to read the Word of God. The Bible says that faith comes by simply hearing Scripture (Romans 10:17). Every time you take the promises and truths in God's Word and declare them out loud, you will be able to sense your faith increasing. Whenever you take God at His Word and trust that it is entirely true, your faith increases.

Praying is another thing you can do to increase your faith. That's because prayer is already an act of faith. It's a way you can reach out and touch God. At one point a woman reached out to the Lord believing that if she just "touched the hem of His garment" she could be healed. Jesus told her that her faith had made her well, and she was healed at that very moment (Matthew 9:20-22). Every time we reach out and touch God in prayer, our lives are healed in some way and our faith is increased.

Every day it becomes more and more crucial that we have faith. There will be times in each of our lives when we will need the kind of faith that is the difference between success or failure, winning or losing, life or death. That's why asking for more faith must be an ongoing prayer. No matter how much faith you have, God can increase it. Even when your faith seems small, you can still speak in faith to the mountains in your life and tell them to move, and God will do the impossible. You can pray for the injured parts of your life to be healed, and God will restore them. You can ask God to increase your faith and give you boldness to act on it, and He will do it.

I Think of God As:
- A supernatural 80-year-old
- A Provider
- A Redeemer
- A Holy Leader
- The Sovereign Lord of all

(Ages 13-15)

What promise of God would you like to claim in faith as your own right now? What prayer would you like to boldly pray in faith and see answered? What would you like to have happen in your life, or in the life of someone you know, that would require a prayer of great faith? Ask God to take the *seed* of faith you have and grow it into a giant *tree* of faith so you can see these things come to pass.

Believe That God Can Set You Free

God has set me free from many things, including alcohol, drugs, fear, depression, anxiety, and unforgiveness, to mention just a few. I have seen the Lord set me free in an instant, and I have also been through a process that took a long time. Regardless of how long it took, what matters most is that it happened. But it didn't happen without faith on my part and the faith of the people who prayed with and for me.

The Main Things I Pray About Are:

- That I will marry the person God has for me
- That I will have godly friends
- That I will feel hopeful and not hopeless
- That God will take away my doubts
- That I can know God better

(Ages 16-19)

We all need to be set free of something at one time or another. That's because no matter how spiritual we are, we're still human. And no matter how perfectly we try to live, we still have an enemy who is trying to erect strongholds of evil in our lives. God wants us to be free from anything that separates us from Him. Jesus taught us to pray, "Deliver us from the evil one" (Matthew 6:13). He would not have said that if we didn't need to be delivered. But so often we don't pray that prayer because we don't have faith in what God says. So often we live our lives as if we don't have faith that Jesus paid an enormous price so we could be free. The Bible says that Jesus "gave Himself for our sins, that He might deliver us from this present evil age, according to the will of our God and Father" (Galatians 1:4).

Do you ever feel distant from God no matter what you do? Does it seem as though your prayers are never being heard or answered? Do you feel discouraged and sad more than you feel the joy of the Lord? Do you find yourself coming back time and again to the same old problems, the same old habits in your actions or thoughts? Do you always feel bad about yourself? If you said yes to any of these questions, I have good news for you. God wants to set you free. But you must have faith that He can and will do it. And you have to pray a prayer of faith.

So often we go along with the devil's plans for our lives, not knowing we don't have to put up with them. Jesus came to lift us above the enemy who wants to destroy us. He wants us to have faith in Him as the Deliverer

I Prayed and God Answered

I prayed because our school is so small. Last Thursday we had a meeting at our school and now a lot of kids will be coming to our school next year.

(Age 13)

and believe that He will set us free from all of that is not His best for our lives. The Bible says, "If the Son makes you free, you shall be free indeed" (John 8:36). That means that no matter how strong that thing is you're struggling with, you must have faith that God's power to deliver you is far stronger.

Worshiping God is a great act of faith. Every time you worship Him, something happens in the spirit realm to break the power of evil. That's because You are in His presence and wherever He is, there is freedom and deliverance. "Now the Lord is the Spirit; and where the Spirit of the Lord is, there is liberty" (2 Corinthians 3:17). Whenever the enemy tries to tell you that you will never get free of something, drown him out with praise. Thank God that He is the Deliverer and you are being delivered even while you are praising Him. The Bible says, "The angel of the LORD encamps all around those who fear Him, and delivers them" (Psalm 34:7).

If it ever seems like you are sliding right back into the very thing you've already been set free of, don't even waste time getting discouraged. Remember that deliverance comes from the Lord, and it is an ongoing process. God does a complete work, and He will see it through to the end. So don't give up because it's taking longer than you hoped. Have faith that "He who has begun a good work in you will complete it until the day of Jesus Christ" (Philippians 1:6).

Believe That Nothing Is Impossible with God

God is the God of the impossible. I have seen that proven true so many times in my life. There would be an impossible situation in which it seemed like there was absolutely no way for things to work out. But I would pray about it, having faith that God hears and answers prayer, and the next morning something major would change and God would do something I never dreamed could happen. He would provide a way through or around the situation, or else He would lift me above it.

My Prayer to God

Lord, I thank You that You said in Your Word that You have a plan for my life, a plan to make me prosperous and successful. I pray that Your will be done in my life, and that I put Your priorities first and not my own. Help me to allow You to lead me in everything I do.

(Age 16)

Whenever you find yourself in an impossible situation, don't let yourself get discouraged or down about it. Go to God right away and pray about it. Tell Him the problem. And then thank Him that there is nothing too hard for Him. Ask Him to establish in you a faith so strong that it doesn't waver, no matter what obstacles, problems, trials, and challenges you face. You will be amazed at how a small seed of faith inside of you can grow into faith that can move a major mountain in your life.

Prayer Power

Lord, increase my faith. Teach me how to "walk by faith, not by sight" (2 Corinthians 5:7). Give me strength to stand strong on Your promises and believe Your every word. I know that "faith comes by hearing, and hearing by the word of God" (Romans 10:17). Make my faith increase every time I hear or read Your Word.

I know that I have been "saved through faith," and that

salvation is a gift from You (Ephesians 2:8). Increase my faith so that I can pray in power. Give me faith to believe for healing every time I pray for the sick. I don't want to see a need and then not have faith strong enough to pray and believe for the situation to change.

Lord, help me "to ask in faith, with no doubting," for "he who doubts is like a wave of the sea driven and tossed by the wind." I know that a doubter is double minded and unstable and will not receive anything from You (James 1:6-8). I know that "whatever is not from faith is sin" (Romans 14:23). I confess any doubt I have as sin before You, and I ask You to forgive me. I don't want to hinder what You want to do in me and through me because of doubt. Increase my faith daily so that I can move mountains for Your glory. In Jesus' name I pray.

WORD POWER

All things are possible to him who believes.

MARK 9:23

Without faith it is impossible to please Him, for he who comes to God must believe that He is, and that He is a rewarder of those who diligently seek Him.

HEBREWS 11:6

In this you greatly rejoice, though now for a little while, if need be, you have been grieved by various trials, that the genuineness of your faith, being much more precious than gold that perishes, though it is tested by fire, may be found to praise, honor, and glory at the revelation of Jesus Christ.

1 PETER 1:6-7

1

What do you especially need to have faith for in your life right now? What mountain or obstacle would you like to see moved?

2

What would you like to see happen in your future that would take a great deal of faith to even pray for? Write it out as a prayer to God and ask Him to increase your faith to believe for it.

3

What great miracle would you like to pray for with regard to the people or situations around you in your world?

chapter 19

'Lord, Help Me'

Know Your Will for My Life

WHEN MY FAMILY AND I MOVED FROM California, we weren't able to sell our house before we left. I didn't want to move in the first place, but after a lot of prayer and inner struggle, I knew in my heart that this move was God's will for us. And I knew we were supposed to move right away and not wait for our house to sell.

Not long after we moved into our new home in Tennessee, a devastating earthquake hit the area where we used to live in California. In fact, our old house was right in the epicenter of the earthquake, which means the impact of the quake was stronger there than anywhere else. The house was so destroyed that it was red-tagged, meaning that it was too dangerous for anyone to even walk into.

When it was safe enough to fly to Los Angeles, I went to see

The Hardest Thing About Prayer Is:

- Thinking of who to pray for
- Taking the time to do it
- Having no one around to listen to me
- Putting it in the right words
- Being out of my comfort zone

(Ages 16-19)

what was left of our former house. The moment I saw what happened to it, I thanked God that no one had been in it when the earthquake hit. If we had not sought God's will for our lives, if we had not listened to Him and did what He directed us to do, we would have been there. And any one of us could have been killed.

In those months after we moved and before the earthquake hit, I had really struggled with the move. It was a lot harder than I thought it would be. I missed my old home and friends terribly. And, frankly, I had been kind of mad at God for making me move. But when I walked through our ruined house, I apologized to God for being so unappreciative of what He had done for us. I told Him I was sorry that I had not trusted Him. That I had not really believed that in His will was the best place to be. That I had fought so hard for *my* way instead of *His.* And that I had complained about my life instead of realizing that His will is always a place of ultimate blessing, even when we can't see it at the moment. If my family and I had not sought the will of God for our lives and followed it, even with reluctance, we would have been there when the earthquake happened.

God's Will Is a Place of Safety

I'm not saying that anyone who was in California during the earthquake was out of the will of God. But I believe that *we* would have been. And I believe that the reason the house did not sell is because anyone who would have been in it at the time would have been seriously injured or killed. When we walk in the will of God, we find safety. When we live outside of God's will, we forfeit His protection.

I Think of God As:
- Always there
- The Creator
- My Friend
- My heavenly Father
- A King

(Ages 13-15)

Always ask God to keep you in the center of His will. Don't choose a college, pursue a career, move to another place, or make any major decision or life change without asking God about it first. And then wait until you know in your heart that it's the will of God before you act on it.

Part of being *protected* by God has to do with obeying Him and living in His will. When you don't do either of those things, you come out from under the umbrella of His protective covering. How many times would people have been spared from something disastrous if they had only asked God to show them what to do and then obeyed Him?

If you pray often, and ask God to always reveal His will to you, He will do that. The Holy Spirit will guide you in all things and speak to your heart. The Bible says, "Your ears shall hear a word behind you, saying, 'This is the way, walk in it,' whenever you turn to the right hand or whenever you turn to the left" (Isaiah 30:21). Never forget that, and you will always walk in a safe place.

Four Things That Are True About God's Will

1. *Following God's will does not mean you won't ever have trouble.* A lot of people think that when you are in the will of God everything goes smoothly. And if everything is not going well, then you must not be in the will of God. But that's not true. Trouble is a part of life. We can't escape it completely, even when we are living right in the center of God's will. But having peace in the middle of the difficulty is what living in God's will is all about. You feel confident when you are certain that you

The Main Things I Pray About Are:

- That I not have lustful feelings
- That our military troops will be safe
- That I will have a long life
- For God's help and guidance
- For finances for me and my family

(Ages 16-19)

are walking in the will of God and doing what He wants you to do. When you're sure of that, you can better deal with what life brings you.

So don't think that trouble in your life means you are out of God's will. God uses the trouble you have to perfect you. There is a big difference between being out of God's will and being pruned or tested by God. Both are uncomfortable, but one leads to life and one doesn't. In one you will have peace, no matter how uncomfortable it gets. In the other, you won't.

2. *Following God's will is not easy.* The life of Jesus confirms that following God's will is not always fun. It is not always pleasant, pain free, and easy. Jesus was doing God's will when He went to the cross. He said, "For I have come down from heaven, not to do My own will, but the will of Him who sent Me" (John 6:38). If anyone could have said, "I don't want to follow God's will today," I think it would have been Him. But He did it perfectly. And now He will enable you to do it too.

3. *Following God's will can make you very uncomfortable.* The truth is that if you don't ever feel stretched or uncomfortable in your walk with the Lord, then I would question whether you are actually *in* the will of God. It has been my personal experience that feeling stretched and uncomfortable is a way of life when walking in the will of God. That's because God will always ask us to do things that our flesh doesn't want to do. He will always ask us to go beyond what makes us feel comfortable. He does that because He wants to know that we are determined to put *His* will above our own will. He wants

us to have the same attitude Jesus had and say, "Not my will, but *Your* will be done, Lord."

4. *Following God's will doesn't happen automatically.* God always gives us a choice as to whether we subject our will to Him or not. We have opportunities to make that decision every day. Will we seek His will? Will we ask Him for wisdom? Will we do what He says? The Bible says, "Do not be unwise, but understand what the will of the Lord is" (Ephesians **5:17**). God's will is the way we choose to live each day of our lives.

Often we don't think we are capable of doing what God is asking us to do, because God will ask us to do things that are beyond ourselves. In other words, they are beyond what we are capable of doing on our own. The reason He does that is because He wants us to depend on Him to help us do it. I could never write a book on my own. Well, maybe I could write enough words to fill one, but I could never do it well enough to get millions of people to buy it. And there is no way I could make a difference in people's lives on my own. But these things happened because I sought God's will about them first. And when He spoke to my heart about what He wanted me to do, I told Him I couldn't do it without His help. I asked Him to work through me to see His will accomplished. And that's what He did.

The Main Things I Pray About Are:
- My band
- My church
- My youth group
- Myself
- Peer pressure
  (Ages 16-19)

God's Will Is for Your Benefit

God's ways are for *your* benefit. His laws are not intended to make you miserable or keep you from having fun. He asks things of you because He knows what is best for you. Trust Him on that.

I Prayed and God Answered

My family and I prayed for my grandpa when he was really sick, and God healed him. He's not saved yet, but we are still speaking to him about it.

(Age 14)

God doesn't want you to live your life for just you, "but for the will of God" (1 Peter 4:2). He wants to "make you complete in every good work to do His will, working in you what is well pleasing in His sight" (Hebrews 13:21). Remember that "it is God who works in you both to will and to do for His good pleasure" (Philippians 2:13). It gives God pleasure when you do His will. It is my prayer that in everything you do "you may stand perfect and complete in all the will of God" (Colossians 4:12).

The best place to start when seeking God's will for your life is by making thanksgiving and praise in your heart a way of life. The Bible says, "In everything give thanks; for this is the will of God in Christ Jesus for you" (1 Thessalonians 5:18). Then pray that God will guide your every step, and thank Him in advance for doing that. If you have done some things you know were not God's will for your life, you need to confess it all to Him and ask Him to lead you back on the path. Being out of God's will can make you absolutely miserable. When you are on the right path and doing what God wants, you will feel good and peaceful and confident. Those feelings alone will cause you to want to do whatever it takes to experience them.

When you live in the center of God's will, you are in a place of safety, protection, blessing, abundance, and peace. Living any other way is just not worth it.

Prayer Power

Lord, I pray You will help me to always know Your will. Give me wisdom and understanding about it (Colossians 1:9). Guide every step I take and help me to walk in a way that pleases You. As I walk close to You each day, show me what I need to do. Like Jesus, I say not my will, but Your will be done in my life. "I delight to do Your will, O my God" (Psalm 40:8). You are more important to me than anything else. Your will is more important to me than my own desires. I want to live as Your servant, doing Your will from my heart (Ephesians 6:6).

Lord, make my heart line up with Yours. Help me to always hear Your voice saying, "This is the way, walk in it." If I am ever doing anything outside of Your will, show me. Speak to me from Your Word so that I will have new understanding. Show me any area of my life where I am not right on target. If there is something I should be doing, reveal it to me so that I can correct my way. I want to move into all You have for me and become all You made me to be by walking in Your perfect will for my life now. In Jesus' name I pray.

WORD POWER

Not everyone who says to Me, "Lord, Lord," shall enter the kingdom of heaven, but he who does the will of My Father in heaven.

MATTHEW 7:21

The world is passing away, and the lust of it; but he who does the will of God abides forever.

1 JOHN 2:17

Trust in the LORD with all your heart, and lean not on your own understanding; in all your ways acknowledge Him, and He shall direct your paths.

PROVERBS 3:5-6

1 Have you ever done something that you know was not the will of God for your life? How did it make you feel? What would you do differently now?

2 In what specific area of your life would you especially like to know the will of God about right now? Write it out as a prayer to God asking Him to show you His will about this issue.

3 Have you ever done something you knew was the will of God for your life, even though it wasn't something you wanted to do? If so, did you feel good knowing you had pleased God? (If you can't think of anything, what about when you get up and go to school or obey your parents or go to church when you want to sleep in on Sunday? That counts.)

chapter 20

"LORD, HELP ME"

Move Into the Future You Have for Me

I WANT YOU TO KNOW THAT THE FUTURE God has for you is greater than anything you can imagine. God says so in His Word. In order to remind you of that, I'm writing this chapter as a personal letter to you so that if you become worried about your future, or you need to be encouraged about what is ahead, you can read it again and again and hopefully hear God speak to your heart.

Dear_____ (fill in your name),

God has a great future for **you**. I know this because He said so. He says **you** have not seen, nor heard, nor have even imagined anything as great as the things He has ahead for **you** (1 Corinthians 2:9). That means **you** have no idea how great **your** future is. But all these good things God has for you in your future are not going to happen automatically. You have to do your part, and then God will do His.

One of the things you have to do is live God's way. This is really very important, because that is the only way your life will work. If you don't live God's way, then you will cut off a lot of the good that God wants to bring into your life. But don't worry about whether you can do everything perfectly. No one can. The Holy Spirit in you will help you to do the right thing if you ask Him to.

Another thing you need to do is to pray about every aspect of your life (Jeremiah 29:11-13). The Holy Spirit in you is God's guarantee that He will help you pray in a way that will cause everything to come to pass that He has promised (Ephesians 1:13-14). Every time you pray and obey God, you are investing in your future.

Although you live in a world where you can't be certain what is going to happen tomorrow, at least you can be certain that God never changes. While you may not know the specific details of what is ahead for you, you can trust that *God* knows. And He will get you safely where you need to go. In fact, the only way to get to the future God has for you is to walk close with Him today.

Remember that walking with God doesn't mean there won't be obstacles in the way. The enemy will see to that. While God has a plan for your future that is good, the devil has one too, and it's not good. He may even come to you and make you think that you don't want to live anymore. If you ever have thoughts like that, please know that they are entirely from the enemy. God created you with the desire, the will, and the instinct to live. Any other thought is from the pit of hell.

Don't fall for it. Recognize it for what it is immediately and praise God that He has given **you** life and a great future.

The devil's plan for **your** life cannot succeed as long as **you** are walking with God, living in obedience to His ways, worshiping only the Lord, standing strong in His Word, and praying about everything. God's plan for **your** life won't happen without a struggle, however, so don't give up when times get tough. Just keep on doing what **you** know is right. Keep asking God to give **you** the strength to do what **you** need to do.

Don't ever judge **your** future by what **you** read in the newspapers, or by any negative words someone has spoken over **you** at one time, or what fearful and negative thoughts the enemy tries to put in **your** brain. **Your** future is in *God's* hands. The only thing that is important is what *He* says about it. He says not to be concerned about **your** future anyway. Instead, be concerned about Him, because *He* is **your** future.

Always remember that **you** are God's child and He loves **you**. So do not become discouraged if **your** prayers don't get answered as fast as **you** would like them to. God hears them and He will answer them in His way and in His timing. Just keep speaking God's Word in faith and don't stop praying. I believe that we are denied certain things for a time because God wants us to pray more. That's because He wants to do something great in response to our prayers, something that can only happen because we are praying a lot.

While it's good to set goals, don't look so far ahead in **your** life that **you** become overwhelmed. **You** have to walk with God a day at a time. Be faithful to do the things **you** have to do today, and let God handle what is ahead. Remember that "the Lord is near to all who call upon Him, to all who call upon Him in truth. He will fulfill the desire of those who fear Him; He also will hear their cry and save them" (Psalm 145:18-19).

The most important thing **you** can do in **your** life is to serve God and serve others. The future God has for **you** includes giving of **yourself**, **your** time, **your** money, **your** knowledge, **your** gifts, or **your** talents to help other people. He says if we don't help others in need, we don't really love Him. Jesus said that "whoever has this world's goods, and sees his brother in need, and shuts up his heart from him, how does the love of God abide in him?" (1 John 3:17). "Let no one seek his own, but each one the other's well-being" (1 Corinthians 10:24). "He who has a generous eye will be blessed, for he gives of his bread to the poor" (Proverbs 22:9). The greatest blessings will come to **you** when **you** ask God to use **you** to touch the lives of others.

You are planting something in **your** life every single day, whether **you** realize it or not. And **you** are also reaping whatever **you** have planted in the past. The quality of **your** life right now is the result of what **you** planted some time before. **You** reap the good and the bad for years after **you** have sown. That's why it is so important to plant the right seeds now.

Jesus said that He is the vine and **you** and I are the branches. If we abide in Him, we will bear fruit (John 15:5). "Abide" means to remain, to stay, to dwell. In other words, if we dwell with Him and He dwells with us, we will bear the fruit of His Spirit (Galatians 5:22-23). That's what we want. Ask God to help **you** plant seeds of love, goodness, kindness, and peace so that is what **you** will have in **your** life. Feed the soil of **your** heart with the food of God's

Word and ask the Holy Spirit to water it every day. As long as you abide faithfully in the true vine, I guarantee you'll produce a crop of spiritual fruit that will make your heavenly Father proud.

God wants to do something great through you. If you are willing to say, "Not my will, but Yours be done, Lord" then He can use you. And He will get you ready to move through the doors He opens for you. Remember, God "is able to do exceedingly abundantly above all that we ask or think, according to the power that works in us" (Ephesians 3:20). He has more for you than you can imagine. So hang on to God and He will help you become all you were created to be and move you into the future He has for you.

Your sister in Christ,

Stormie Omartian

Prayer Power

Lord, I put my future in Your hands and ask that You would give me total peace about it. I don't want to be trying to make my future happen with my own plans. I want to be in the center of Your plans, knowing that You will give me all that I need for what is ahead. I pray You would give me strength to stand strong without giving up. Help me to run the race so that I will finish strong and receive the prize You have for me (1 Corinthians 9:24).

Help me to plant good seeds in my life so that what I reap is good. Help me to always abide in You. Plant the fruit of Your Spirit in me—the love, joy, peace, longsuffering, kindness, goodness, faithfulness, gentleness, and self-control—and cause it to flow through me to others (Galatians 5:22-23). Thank You for Your promise that if I abide in You and Your Word abides in me, I can ask what I desire and it will be done for me (John 15:7). I invite You, Holy Spirit, to fill me afresh today, for I know that without You I can do nothing.

Lord, make me all You created me to be and help me do something great for Your kingdom and Your glory. I humble myself under Your mighty hand, O God, knowing that You will lift me up in due time. I cast all my cares upon You, knowing that You care for me and will not let me fall (1 Peter 5:6-7). I reach out for Your hand today so I can walk with You into the future You have for me. In Jesus' name I pray.

WORD POWER

I know the thoughts that I think toward you, says the LORD, thoughts of peace and not of evil, to give you a future and a hope. Then you will call upon Me and go and pray to Me, and I will listen to you. And you will seek Me and find Me, when you search for Me with all your heart.

JEREMIAH 29:11-13

Whatever you ask in My name, that I will do, that the Father may be glorified in the Son. If you ask anything in My name, I will do it.

JOHN 14:13-14

Arise, shine; for your light has come! And the glory of the LORD is risen upon you. For behold, the darkness shall cover the earth, and deep darkness the people; but the LORD will arise over you, and His glory will be seen upon you.

ISAIAH 60:1-2

1 What would you like to see happen in your future?

2 Do you have any fears about the future? If so, what are they? Write out a prayer asking God to take those fears away.

3 Write out a prayer asking God to bless the dreams you have for your future that are His will for your life, and take away the ones that are not His will for you.

A Young Man After God's Own Heart
By Jim George
Jim George takes older teenagers on a radical journey of faith.
Through God's extreme wisdom and powerful insights from the life
of warrior and leader King David, young men will discover biblical
principles that blaze a trail to godly living.

A Young Woman After God's Own Heart
By Elizabeth George
In this book written just for them, teen girls will discover God's priorities for their lives—including prayer, submission, faithfulness, and
joy—and how to embrace those priorities in daily life.

A Young Woman's Call to Prayer
By Elizabeth George
Elizabeth George offers another exciting teen book—*A Young
Woman's Call to Prayer.* From her own journey, the Bible, and the lives
of others, Elizabeth reveals the explosive power and dynamic impact
of prayer on everyday life.

The Bondage Breaker® Youth Edition
By Neil Anderson and Dave Park
Helping teens strip away superficiality and live Christ-centered lives,
Neil and Dave offer steps for breaking sinful habits; increasing confidence that through Christ sin wields no power; and relying on the
Holy Spirit for guidance.